Brazil, the River Plate, and the Falkland Islands

DN PEDRO II EMPERADOR DEL BRASIL

BRAZIL,
THE RIVER PLATE,

AND THE

FALKLAND ISLANDS;

WITH THE CAPE HORN ROUTE TO AUSTRALIA

INCLUDING NOTICES OF

LISBON, MADEIRA, THE CANARIES, AND CAPE VERDS.

BY

WILLIAM HADFIELD,

MANY YEARS RESIDENT IN BRAZIL, AND SECRETARY TO THE SOUTH AMERICAN AND GENERAL
STEAM NAVIGATION COMPANY.

ILLUSTRATED, BY PERMISSION, FROM THE SOUTH AMERICAN SKETCHES OF

SIR W. GORE OUSELEY, K.C.B.,

LATE HER MAJESTY'S MINISTER PLENIPOTENTIARY TO THE STATES OF LA PLATA, AND FORMERLY
CHARGE D'AFFAIRES AT THE COURT OF BRAZIL

AND, BY PERMISSION, FROM THE DRAWINGS OF

SIR CHARLES HOTHAM, K.C.B.,

DURING HIS RECENT

MISSION TO PARAGUAY,

OF WHICH COUNTRY MUCH NEW INFORMATION IS SUPPLIED, AS ALSO OF

THE REGION OF THE AMAZON.

PORTRAITS, MAPS, CHARTS, AND PLANS.

LONDON:
LONGMAN, BROWN, GREEN, AND LONGMANS.
1854.

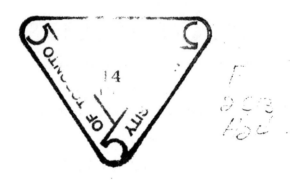

LONDON:
JOHN CASSELL, PRINTER,
LUDGATE-HILL.

CONTENTS.

PAGE

EXPLANATORY PREFACE.

Steam requirements of Anglo South American commerce anterior to 1850 How supplied then Inadequacy of means to the general end, and to Lancastrian ends in particular Subsequent supply Liverpool still left out Chartered liberty to help itself, and the consequence thereof Paddle pioneer of the ocean fleet to the Plate Dates and distances in a new line What may be done by putting on the screw for three months Fifteen thousand miles of steaming, with the Author's notes thereon, and suggestions for the same being continued by other people Epilogue apologetic. 1

INTRODUCTION

Cursory retrospect of South American discoveries Their difficulties then, how to be estimated at present. Their interest to this age as compared with that of ancient conquests Cruelties of the early invaders Retributive visitations Columbus and his cotemporaries Cortez and the conquest of Mexico Subsequent position of the country Santa Anna, his antecedents and prospects Pizarro in Peru, and his Lieutenant, Almagro, in Chili Condition of those republics since and now their past gold and present guano Modern commanders in those countries Predominance of the Irish element in the fray The O'Learys and O'Higginses in the Andes. San Martin and his aid-de-camp, O'Brien, and his auxiliary, M'Cabe The Portuguese discoverers Magellan and his Straits, and Peacock's steaming to the Pacific three hundred years afterwards Cabral and Brazil De Gama and the Cape, and Camoens' celebration of the achievement Enrichment of the Iberian Peninsula from these causes Subsequent impoverishment of mother countries and colonies Exceptional position of Brazil in this respect, and reason thereof Different results in North America, and why Imperfect knowledge in Europe of South America Works thereon Characteristics of the several authorities Prescott, Southey, Koster, Gardner, Humboldt, Dr Dundas, Woodbine Parish, M'Cann, Edwards, Maury, and others Want of information still on Paraguay, and the region of the Amazon. Object of this volume to supply that void Aim of the Author not political, but commercial 8

CHAP I —LIVERPOOL TO LISBON

Illustrations—The Argentina on her maiden voyage	Praca do Commercio, Lisbon.
Belem Castle, mouth of the Tagus	Cintra, near Lisbon
	Palace of Adjuda

The Argentina on her maiden voyage Capacity and capability of the river boat at sea. From the Mersey to the Tagus in four days Lord Carnarvon on Mafra and its marble halls. Aspect and Attributes of the Lusitanian Capital and its Vicinage Portuguese Millers and the grinding process among the grain growers. Native memorabilia of the earthquake, and Anglo reminiscence thereof The lac poet of Tom Jones, and eke of Roderick Random Portuguese peculiarities Personal and political economy Fiscal fatuities. Market-place notabilia Lisbon society Clubs and Cookery Tea and turn-out. Friars, females, and fashions Lusitanian fidalgos, or Portuguese peers in parliament. Portugal the Paradise of protectionists and poverty. Free Trade the only corrective of such calamities Court circulars,

Conventions, and Commanders — Few books about Portugal, and necessity for more. Hints from the newest, including the Oliveira prize essay — Diplomatic and consular memoranda 35

CHAP II —LISBON TO MADEIRA.
Illustration—The Laurel Tree.

Two more days' pleasant paddling on the ocean — Approach to Madeira. Charming aspect of the island — Unique boats and benevolent boatmen — Pastoral progression in bucolic barouches extraordinary — Personal appearance of the inhabitants — Atmospheric attractions of Madeira, and absence of all natural annoyances — The vine-blight and its consequences, present and prospective, on the people at home and the consumption of their wine abroad — Funchal, and its urban and suburban et ceteras — Romance and reality of the history of the island — 'Once Upon a Time' — Importance of English residents to the place — Cost of living, and what you get for your money — Royal and illustrious visitors — Mercantile matters, and consular cordiality — Grave reflections in the British burial-ground 65

CHAP III —MADEIRA TO CAPE VERDS
Illustration—Interior of Hotel, Teneriffe.

Oceanic sailing again — Halcyon weather, and modern steaming to the Fortunatæ Insulæ of the ancients. A stare on the saffron-coloured singing birds — Touching Teneriffe, and Miltonic parallel to the Arch-Enemy — Approach to Porto Grande, and what we found there, especially its extensive accommodation for steamers — Deficiency of water the one drawback — Something concerning Ethiopic Serenaders under the line — Promethean promontory extraordinary — A memento of mortality midway in the world — Portuguese rewards honourably earned by an Englishman — Utility of Consuls in such places — First acquaintance with an earthquake — Verd grapes soured by a paternal government — Interchange of news between the Outward and the Homeward bound — A good propelling turn towards a brother of the screw 74

CHAP IV —CAPE ST VINCENT TO PERNAMBUCO

Progress from Porto Grande to Pernambuco — Steam triumphs against trade wind — Further superiority of screw over sail — The Argentina in a south-wester — Apropos of malaria, and something sanitary about Brazil — The yellow fever whence comes it, and what has become of it — Quarrels about quarantine — Brazil in advance of the old country in these matters 82

CHAP V —EMPIRE OF BRAZIL.
Illustration—Entrance to Pernambuco Harbour

Rather prefatory and not very particular, though somewhat personal — Books on Brazil should be in the Medium Viam for the present route, avoiding the Scylla of extreme succinctness and the Charybdis of needless diffuseness — Object of the author to attain the golden medium — With what success, gentle reader, say? — Discovery of the country by the Portuguese — Their subsequent disputes with, and final expulsion of, the Dutch — Extent and population, variety of soil and produce — Difficulty of communication between the provinces and the capital, in consequence of the extreme distance and imperfect means of travelling — Extraordinary instance of the round-about nature of news circulating in Brazil some time ago — Steam corrective of such sluggishness — A glance at the Brazilian littoral, beginning with the Amazon, and ending with Rio Grande do Sul — Pará and its productions — Rio Negro, and its recent political elevation — Maranham and its mercantile importance. Laird's steam leveller, on the singular stream of the Itapecuru — Justice for England by Maranham magistrates. Piauhy and its products, also Ceara, Rio Grande do Norte, and Paraiba — Pernambuco revisited by the writer, and welcomed with a rythmetical sentimental something concerning 'Long, long ago!' 88

CONTENTS.   iii

                                                                      PAGE
                        CHAP. VI.—PERNAMBUCO.

Illustrations—Pernambuco | De Mornay's Patent Cane Mill.
Chora Meninas |

"That strain again!" 'It hath a dying fall' 'Auld Lang Syne, or 'tis thirty years
ago' Aspect of Pernambuco from the sea Tripartite division of the city, Recife,
St Antonio, and Boa Vista Note on the old town of Olinda and its new namesake, the steamer No 2 of this A 1 line March of improvement by land and sea,
in respect to ships and city Such Brazilian progress a lesson for West Indians.
Frugality and personal activity on the one hand, prodigality and vicarial mismanagement on the other, being the real difference between the position of the planters
in either place Sugar-manufacturing improvements De Mornay's patent cane-
crushing mill, and its merits Exports of Pernambuco to United States Peculiarities of the soil, population, and produce Hygienic hints to the consumptive and
the yellow-feverish Initiation of the railway era, by the De Mornays, in Pernambuco, and the immense importance of the proposed line Mr Borthwick's report on
the project, and the writer's anticipation of its success   100

                    CHAP. VII.—ALAGOAS AND SEREGIPE.

Area, products, and population of Alagoas Maceio, the principal seaport. Rivers
navigable only by boats, except the San Francisco. Primitive condition of the
province of Seregype, and prospects of rapid improvement through railways.   117

                        CHAP. VIII.—BAHIA.

Illustrations—Entrance to the port | Chapel of San Goncalo, Bahia.
of Bahia |

Bahia, its old name retained in a new place the province and the city, present condition and splendid prospects of both Intra-mural peculiarities and extra-mural
properties Prolific sugar produce Historic, artistic, and archaeological attractions of Bahia Souvenirs of the Jesuits Relics of St Ignatius Loyola and St
Francis Xavier A Bahian church built in Europe British Bahian clergyman
and local railways Health of the city A Brazilian poet warbling native wood-
notes very wild Necessity for keeping a nautical eye in fine frenzy rolling towards
the Abrolhos Departure from Bahia, and approach to the Brazilian capital Notes 120

                        CHAP. IX.—RIO JANEIRO.

Illustrations—Entrance to the Harbour | Aqueduct and Convent of St Teresa.
Organ Mountains and Sugar-loaf Rock. | Falls of Itamarity.
Convent of Nossa Senora da Penha |

Night upon the waters, and daybreak on the land Beauty of the approaches Appre-
hended retrogression, but real progression, in the city The stay mania in the tropics,
and some of its consequences Notes on carriages, operas, snuff-taking, polking
washerwomen, blacks, whites, odds and ends, and things in general, original and
imported. Social, sanitary, and governmental matters of divers kinds. Composition
of the Brazilian Chambers, and business therein. State of parties Abolition of the
slave trade. Sittings of the senate. No necessity for Mr. Brotherton in the Brazils.
Character of the present Emperor Wreck of the Pernambucano Heroism of a
black sailor Rigorous regulations of the Rio custom-house Suggestions for the
extension of Brazilian commerce, and the prevention of smuggling Revisal of the
Brazilian tariff Educational progress since 1808 French literature and fashion
Provisions in the Rio market Monkeys and lizards articles of food Oranges,
bananas, chirimoyas, and granadillas Difficulties of the labour question since the
suppression of the slave-trade Character of the Indians State of feeling as regards the coloured people Negro emancipation 'looming in the future.' An experimental trip on the Rio and Petropolis railway.   136

CONTENTS.

PAGE

MEMOIR OF ADMIRAL GRENFELL.

Illustration—Portrait of Admiral Grenfell. 185

CHAP. X.—THE AMAZON.

Sources of the Maranon. Rapids and cataracts. Embouchures of the Amazon. Its volume, compared with the Ganges and the Brahmapootra. Its discovery by Pinzon. Expedition of Orellana. Gold-seeking expedition of Pedro de Orsua. Settlement of Pará, and discovery of the Rio Negro. The missions of the Jesuits, and their expulsion. Discovery of the communication between the Amazon and the Orinoco. Revolution of 1835. Pará: its streets and public buildings. Explorations of M. Castelnau and Lieutenant Herndon. Tributaries and settlements of the Tocantins. Lieutenant Gibbon's exploration of the Madera. His interview with General Belzu. What is wanted to turn the stream of tropical South American commerce eastward. Herndon's descent of the Huallaga, Tarapoto, and its future prospects. Chasuta: its trade with Lima and Pará. Yurimaguas, and the Cachiyacu. Steamboat communication between Nauta and Pará. Progress of a piece of cotton from Liverpool to Sarayacu. Estimated cost and profit of steam vessels on the Amazon. Trade of Egas. The new province of Amazonas. Exports of Barra. The Rio Negro and its tributaries. Communication by the Cassiquiari between the Amazon and the Orinoco. Productions of Amazonas. Santarem. The Tapajos, and its tributaries. Rapids of the Pará and the Xingú. Climate and products of Pará. Benefits to be expected from the opening of the Amazon and European immigration. 193

DR. DUNDAS ON BRAZIL: ITS CLIMATE AND PEOPLE.

Salubrity of the Climate. Causes of, proofs of, objections to. Northern, southern, and central provinces. Equability of temperature. Heat, humidity, rain, winds, electricity, hail, ice. Tropical heat and light. Influence on Europeans. Acclimatization. Increase of certain diseases. Yellow fever; its probable disappearance. Physical, social, moral, and religious condition of the people. Prophylactic measures. 214

CHAP. XI.—MONTE VIDEO.

Illustrations—Portrait of Sir W. G. Ouseley, K.C.B.	The Stray Cow.
The Lasso.	View of Monte Video.
	Milk at a rial a glass.

First impressions of the Uruguayan capital unfavourable. The New Custom House. An instance of enterprise without prudence. Commercial advantages of Monte Video. Prosperity obtained at the expense of Buenos Ayres. Revisal of the Buenos Ayrean tariff. Alluvial deposits of the Rio Plata. Gas from mares' grease. Traces of a siege. Unprofitable ploughing by Oribe's projectiles. Condition of the Streets. The horses of La Plata, and the Lasso. Commerce of London with Monte Video and Buenos Ayres. Mules for the Australian gold diggings. Diminution of the Customs. Bitter fruits of British and French intervention. Sir William Gore Ouseley and the British Loan. The market-place. Italian boatmen. Encouragement to foreigners. Aspect of the environs. The latest revolution. Sketch of the history of Monte Video. 229

CHAP. XII.—BUENOS AYRES.

Illustrations—View of Buenos Ayres.	May-day in Buenos Ayres.
Quinta, or country house.	La Plaza Victoria.
View from the terrace of the quinta.	Palermo.
Negro laundresses at Buenos Ayres.	Apothecary's shop.
View on the river.	Going to mass.

CONTENTS

PAGE

Departure from Monte Video Streets and buildings of the Argentine capital The climate and the people. Prohibition of the slave trade Characters of the dictator and his successor, Urquiza Argentine Confederation Foreign intervention and capture of Rosas' fleet Capitulation of General Oribe, and fall of Rosas Fluvial obstructions to trade and navigation English residents Railway projects. South American debate Foreign shopkeepers and Irish servants General Paz . 260

MEMORANDA ON ROSAS, URQUIZA, AND THE PAMPAS.

Illustration —Portraits of Generals Rosas and Urquiza 290

CHAP XIII —UP THE PARANA.

Illustrations—Rosario | Corrientes.
San Nicolas |

Preparations for an experimental trip up the Parana Captain Sullivan's descent of the river at a terrific pace Island of Martin Garcia Note on the confluents of the Rio Plata A Scotch experimental philosopher in Corrientes Alluvial deposits at the delta of the Parana Signs of progress in the interior An American pioneer of civilization The steamer aground, and fired upon Moonlight on the river and the woods Geographical note on the Parana and the Plata. Obligado and San Nicolas Mr Mackinnon's description of the scenery Arrival at Rosario Multifarious applications of hides and horns Descent of the river, and arrival at Martin Garcia Corrientes and the gauchos Difficulties of the navigation, and a word about the Uruguay 305

CHAP XIV —PARAGUAY

Illustrations—Portrait of Sir Charles | View near Assumption
Hotham, K C B | Church of the Recoleta
View of Assumption | Portrait of General Lopez

Sources of information General Pacheco Inaccuracies of Sir Woodbine Parish Navigability of the Parana by large vessels Decrees of the government of Paraguay on the treatment of foreigners Decrees relative to inventions and improvements Mr Drabble's commercial mission, and its results Cultivation of cotton Drawbacks to its extension Scarcity of labour. Provisions of the treaty between Great Britain and Paraguay. The commercial resources of that country little known in this. Navigability of the Paraguay and the Uruguay Obligation of the Brazilian and Buenos Ayrean governments to remove impediments Population of Paraguay Public works undertaken by the Consular Government Salubrity of the climate. Fertility of the soil. Pasturage illimitable Character of the Paraguayans President Lopez. Diplomatic mission of Sir Charles Hotham General Lopez State of the country at the death of Francia. First measures of the Consular Government Revenue of Paraguay. Administration of justice. Revision of the tariff Release of political prisoners at the termination of Francia's Reign of Terror. Anticipations of intercourse with Europe 328

MEMOIR OF SIR CHARLES HOTHAM, K C B.

CHAP. XV —HOMEWARD BOUND.

Illustration—The Brazileira on her homeward voyage.

Departure from Buenos Ayres. Arrival at Monte Video. Guano deposits of Patagonia Bahia Blanca Eligibility of the district for an overland route to Chili Chilian grant for direct steam communication with England. Accessions to steam navigation on the Brazilian coast. Opening of the Amazon. Departure from Monte Video.

CONTENTS.

PAGE

Rough wind and heavy sea — Aspect of Raza under various lights and shades — Hotel accommodation of Rio Janeiro — A wet day at Bahia — Consular memoranda on Venezuela, Bolivia, and Equador — Arrival at Pernambuco — Meeting with the Olinda — Arrival at Porto Grande — Seven days' steaming against the wind — Madeira in the distance — Arrival at Belem — Miseries and absurdities of the quarantine system — Towing the pilot astern — Passage up St George's Channel. Arrival in the Mersey — Loss of the Olinda and the Argentina — New ocean and river steamers 359

THE FALKLAND ISLANDS

Advantages presented as a convict settlement, as place of re-fit for merchantmen, and a naval depôt — The Corporation of the Falkland Islands' Company — Healthiness of the climate — The abundance of fresh water — Cost of transport less than that to other colonies — Geographical position and extent — Distance from the Main — The small naval force required — Causes of insecurity at other settlements not found here — Their detachment a provision against escape — Guard less required here than elsewhere — The cheapness of provisions how supplied — Employment — The gradual supply of convicts not requisite — How first comers may be disposed of — Smallness of preliminary outlay, and its speedy return — Opinions of various servants of the Crown — Two propositions — The riddance of convicts — Relief to the mother country — Redemption of the pledge made to convicts — Facilities for reformation — Restoration of the penitent to society without risk to the innocent — Agricultural school for juvenile convicts — Complete depôt for naval re-fit near Cape Horn — Saving of port charges and of freight — Easy performance of ships' repairs, if patent slip laid down — Secure coaling station for steamers — First-rate naval station — 'key of the Pacific' in time of war — Testimony of Governor Rennie and Captain Matthews of the Great Britain   376

EXPLANATORY PREFACE.

Steam Requirements of Anglo South American commerce anterior to 1850 —How supplied then —Inadequacy of Means to the General End, and to Lancastrian Ends in particular —Subsequent Supply —Liverpool still left out —Chartered Liberty to help itself, and the consequences thereof —Paddle Pioneer of the Ocean Fleet to the Plate —Dates and Distances in a new Line —What may be done by putting on the Screw for Three Months —Fifteen Thousand Miles of Steaming, with the Author's Notes thereon, and Suggestions for the same being continued by other people —Epilogue apologetic

UNTIL 1850, the Eastern coast of South America, including the extensive and flourishing empire of Brazil, and the boundless regions watered by the La Plata and its tributaries, were entirely without European steam navigation. The old process of sailing-ships, and a monthly sailing-packet from Falmouth, conveying mails, were the only medium of communication. In that year, the Royal Mail Company entered upon the service they had undertaken with government, to run a monthly steamer from Southampton to Rio Janeiro, and a branch steamer to the River Plate. The vessels placed on the station were drafted from their West India fleet; and, although not possessed of extraordinary steaming or sailing qualities, they performed the voyage with regularity, and in a space of time which reduced to one half that ordinarily occupied by the sailing-craft. The consequence was an augmentation of traffic, both of goods and passengers, such as few persons contemplated, and the line proved speedily unequal to the task of dealing with either to the extent required. Moreover, it was found that one very important feature in the case, a direct traffic with the River Plate, was quite unprovided for, and no provision whatever made by which goods and merchandize could be forwarded thither, the branch steamer from Rio Janeiro only taking passengers. But, even had mercantile necessities in this direction been supplied, there was a strong feeling that Liverpool, as the emporium of British trade with South America, ought to possess a steam-line of its own, and that goods and passengers should not be compelled to find their way to Southampton. The great manufacturing districts which have Liverpool for their seaport supply at least seven-eighths of the entire trade to South America,* and it seemed an anomaly that no direct steam communication should exist between them. Accordingly, in 1851, parties connected with the district, having organized a company, went before the Board of Trade for a royal charter, alleging, as a reason for such concession, the importance of our interests in the quarter named, the necessity of more frequent intercourse since steam had been established, and that once a month was not sufficient for wants so extensive and pressing. These arguments,

---

* In reference to the preponderating interest of Liverpool in this trade, an influential metropolitan journalist, commenting on the treaty with Paraguay soon after its ratification in London, observes —

Liverpool is the very centre and focus of our foreign trade. There almost every man you meet is either engaged in commerce, or is in the service of those so engaged. Liverpool, like the seat of the Pope of Rome—but in a widely different sense—has its agents and its commercial missionaries in every climate and in every latitude, and there is not one among them who is not as intent and energetic in his work as those 'soldiers of the faith,' whom Rome sent out on the South American missions in the two centuries from 1535 to 1735. The fiery enthusiasm of Don Pedro de Mendoza himself, who offered Charles V to complete the conquest of Paraguay and the Rio de la Plata at his own expense, is equalled by some of those indomitable agents of the counting-house, who are as zealous for commercial conquests as the Andalusian Hidalgo was for the aggrandisement of his Sovereign and master. We doubt that even Father Charlevoix himself, so often cited and praised by his brother Breton, Chateaubriand, and who has given us six volumes of a charming history of Paraguay—which he explored in person—exhibited more zeal for the interests of his order in the countries watered by the Rio de la Plata, the Rio Salado, the Rio Negro, the Catapuliche, and the Rio de la Encarnacion, than do those Liverpool junior partners, clerks, and supercargoes, who are charged with the interests of considerable commercial houses in such distant latitudes   *   *   *   *
Through the rivers opened to us by the efforts of Lord Malmesbury, one-fourth, at least, of the produce of South America, must be brought to the market of the world, and of this commerce Liverpool will certainly have the largest, and Bristol, Glasgow, and London, a considerable share.

EXPLANATORY PREFACE.

backed, as they were, by memorials from Liverpool, Manchester, and other places, had weight with Her Majesty's Government, and a charter of incorporation was obtained. The directors immediately proceeded to contract for the building of suitable steamers, but delay, caused by unusual pressure of work, somewhat retarded intended operations.*

On the 27th of August, 1853, the company's first, or pioneer, steamer intended for the River Plate station, sailed from Liverpool, and was followed on the 24th of September by the ocean steamer, Brazileira, Captain Daniel Green, who had long com-

* In the original prospectus of the company, whose calculations, apart from two wrecks, as to the performances of their vessels have since been so well verified by experience, it was stated that, 'The importance and extent of our trade with Brazil and the River Plate, and the necessity which exists for a more perfect postal communication with these countries, mainly suggested this enterprise; and, accordingly, the first efforts of this company will be devoted, not only to supply the desideratum of a bi-monthly mail, but to afford to shippers of goods a cheap and speedy conveyance, which the acceleration of the mails over the old system of sailing packets renders most desirable; the tonnage at present employed in the Rio and River Plate trades, from the Port of Liverpool alone amounts to 30,000 tons annually, while the value of exports, principally consisting of Manchester and other similar fabrics, is upwards of three millions sterling per annum. The number of first class passengers was, until the establishment of the mail steamers, very circumscribed; but since that period it has materially increased, not less than one hundred per month, each way, being now the average. Of the second class of passengers and the lower description of emigrants the numbers who have gone from Great Britain and the continent, by sailing vessels, has been very great, more than is generally supposed, not fewer than 4,000 persons having emigrated to Rio Grande and the southern ports of Brazil during the last year, while to the River Plate the numbers for years past has been still more considerable; and the inducements held out to emigrants in both countries are so great, that, with the additional facilities afforded by a regular steam communication, a largely progressive increase may be fairly calculated on. Thus it will be seen that a large field is open for this company's operations, and, as the rates of passage proposed to be charged are extremely moderate, being within what has hitherto been obtained by sailing ships, it is not unreasonable to suppose that the estimate of the number of passengers, upon which the requisite calculations are based, is under what may fairly be expected from this country, the continent, and Portugal. Three steam-ships, of from 1,500 to 1,700 tons, and about 300 horse-power, will, in the first instance, be built for the Rio line. The vessels will be modelled after the most approved principles, and, with the ample power proposed, it is confidently anticipated that an average speed of at least 10 knots per hour will

manded clipper vessels in the Brazil trade. As secretary to the company, and possessing a local knowledge of Brazil, it was thought desirable that the author should proceed in the Argentina, for the purpose of seeing that proper arrangements were made at the ports of call for their vessels, and to obtain from foreign governments the facilities and assistance requisite to carry on a steam company of this magnitude with any success The voyage was accomplished in a little more than three months, the writer having returned to Liverpool, by the Brazileira, on the 5th of November, during which time he had gone over nearly 15,000 miles of distance (including a trip up the Parana), spent a fortnight at Rio Janeiro, and three weeks in the River Plate, besides calling at all the stations both ways, namely, outwards—Lisbon, Madeira, St. Vincent. Pernambuco, and Bahia; and, homewards—Bahia, Pernambuco, St Vincent, and Lisbon, which latter is to be the track of the regular ocean line, subject to modifications. &c

Thus, it will be seen, from this brief recapitulation of dates and distances, that in the space of two months a merchant can visit his Brazil establishment, and another, under three months, can look after his River Plate affairs, often saving himself much anxiety and loss of time. The manufacturer can, without great trouble, make himself practically acquainted with the markets he wishes to trade to ; the botanist and naturalist can quickly be transported to the virgin ground of Paraguay, or, now that the Brazilian government have placed contract steamers on the greatest of all great rivers, may ascend the Amazon, with like certainty of reward as novel and varied, and depend on a prompt return of his newly acquired specimens Whilst, which is equally important,

be attained. The branch boat will be of smaller dimensions, suitable for the navigation of the River Plate It is calculated that the passage to Rio will not exceed twenty-five days, and that the whole distance to the River Plate will be accomplished in thirty-five days, including the needful detention in Rio to transfer the cargo and passengers to the branch boat. The average passages of the best ships at present employed is not less than fifty days to Rio, and sixty to the River Plate ' The branch boat, it will be seen hereafter, was lost, as likewise the Olinda, the second ship of the Ocean line, both, however, having been replaced.

the natives of those countries have an opportunity of visiting Europe, and forming, by personal contact, those relations of amity and good will which tend so much to soften prejudices, and bring about a right understanding on all points mutually advantageous Hence the ramifications of such enterprises as steam are most interesting in their results to mankind; and, if once the tide of emigration begins to set in fairly towards that immense agricultural field watered by the rivers of South America, there is no foreseeing the extension of wealth and prosperity that must assuredly follow; for population is the sole requirement to fit these limitless and teeming regions to work out the destiny which it is impossible to doubt that Providence, in the fulness of time, has designed for that portion of the earth, where the majesty and the luxuriance of nature invite the presence of man through highways at once the mightiest and most facile in the world.

A desire to place these objects forcibly before the public is the origin of this work. Though conscious of its imperfections and short-comings, the writer would guard against the imputation of impertinence in offering it as the result merely of the experience derived from the rapid run out and home indicated in the remarks just preceding. He is no book-maker; though he ventures to hope that his book will, in some degree, fill a vacuum left by certain recent accomplished professors of that branch of the fine arts in this department of travellers' information for the untravelled public. The several topics discussed in the ensuing pages have been the subject-matter of his earnest consideration for many years Long resident in South America, and familiar with its commercial necessities, his attention had naturally been directed to all the mercantile points embraced in the old circle of communication with Europe, while the circumstances of his position, in connection with a new enterprise, enabled him to contemplate matters in a somewhat novel light; and he was peculiarly fortunate in deriving his knowledge of the recent interesting diplomatic and commercial incidents in the Upper Parana and the Paraguay on the spot, and from the most competent sources.

Assiduously availing of these and all others of a like kind whenever they presented themselves,—which was not unfrequently—he has, wherever practicable, rendered the expression of his own remarks subordinate to the main design of bringing together whatever data should serve to make his volume useful as an exposition, at one view, of the present condition, primarily, of the East Coast and the Amazon and Platine interior, and, incidentally, of South America generally—an object embraced in no other single publication of this class. He is well aware that a complete embodiment of such a design would tax powers far higher and opportunities more varied than his. But he will be content, if, in succeeding a little, he should be the means of stimulating others to achieve a great deal more in a like direction.

Though necessarily containing little that is new, the *resumé* of discoveries, prefixed to the opening chapter, is offered as likely to be serviceable in recalling to the elder reader some of the more salient facts he already knows, but which are necessary to be repeated, and in suggesting to the younger student of South American history,—than which it is hardly possible to name any more exciting, delightful, or instructive,—those sources that will render him easily cognizant of what has been written on the several branches of the subject up to the present date. A similar justification, it is hoped, will serve for the seeming surplusage of the remarks under the head of Lisbon, Madeira, and the Verds; though it will be found that the chapters devoted to those well-known places contain a good deal of fresh information calculated to be acceptable to all calling at the several ports.

Often observing the inconvenience experienced by South Americans coming to England, and by Englishmen proceeding to South America, from unacquaintance with the names and residences of the respective diplomatic and consular agents in both countries, the author has been at some pains to collect the necessary information on this head; and, as regards the antecedents of the English officials, has relied upon that very useful manual, the 'Foreign Office List for 1854,' by Mr. F. W. H. Cavendish, *Précis*

Writer to the Earl of Clarendon. The large map of South America has been expressly prepared for this volume, chiefly with a view to exhibit the river navigation affected by the late treaties, and will be found, I have every reason to believe, much the most correct that has yet been published of the whole continent; for, generally speaking, maps of South America, or of any portion of it, are ludicrously inaccurate. The map of the growingly important settlement of the Falkland Islands has likewise been adapted from the most recent surveys, and is calculated to prove of benefit to captains making the homeward Australian voyage by Cape Horn.

Claughton, Birkenhead,
    March 30, 1854

INTRODUCTION.

Cursory Retrospect of South American Discoveries —Their difficulties then, how to be estimated at present —Their interest to this age as compared with ancient conquests —Cruelties of the early invaders —Retributive visitations —Columbus and his cotemporaries —Cortez and the conquest of Mexico —Subsequent position of the country —Santa Anna, his antecedents and prospects —Pizarro in Peru, and his Lieutenant, Almagro, in Chili —Condition of those Republics since and now: their past gold and present guano —Modern commanders in those countries —Predominance of the Irish element in the fray —The O'Learys and O'Higginses in the Andes —San Martin and his aid-de-camp, O'Brien, and *his* auxiliary, M'Cabe —The Portuguese discoverers —Magellan and his Straits, and Peacock's steaming to the Pacific three hundred years afterwards —Cabra, and Brazil —De Gama and the Cape, and Camoens' celebration of the achievement.—Enrichment of the Iberian Peninsula from these causes —Subsequent impoverishment of mother countries and colonies —Exceptional position of Brazil in this respect, and reason thereof —Different results in North America, and why —Imperfect knowledge in Europe of South America —Works thereon —Characteristics of the several authorities: Prescott, Southey, Koster, Gardner, Humboldt, Dr Dundas, Woodbine Parish, M'Cann, Edwards, Maury, and others —Want of information still on Paraguay and the region of the Amazon —Object of this Volume to supply that void.—Aim of the Author not Political, but Commercial

NEARLY four centuries have rolled past since the great discoveries of Columbus and his followers led to the establishment of Spanish and Portuguese dominion over the vast continent of South

America, and were succeeded somewhat later by the still more important settlement of the Anglo-Saxon race on the northern portion of the New World.* These events, marvellous in themselves and in their accessories, and momentous from the way in which they have affected the destinies of the human race, present a study singularly and enduringly interesting, differing so strongly as they do from the characteristics of ancient history. The latter are necessarily contemplated by the reader as types and symbols of the past, on which he has only the privilege of reflecting; whilst in the former case, in perusing the story of these comparatively modern discoveries of hitherto unknown continents, he feels himself almost a sharer in the adventures of those extraordinary men by whose deeds his own present destiny is so essentially influenced. He cannot desire to be a Lycurgus or a Phocion, a Cæsar or a Cato; but it is no tax on the imagination, no repulse to the feeling, to picture himself a Columbus in embryo, and his soul and being is wrapt up in the narrative of that great voyager. The English are proverbially a nautical people, nursed and cradled in the lap of that ocean with whose element their earliest sympathies are enlisted and identified. In these days it is a light matter indeed, with the facilities of progression abounding on all sides, and the great ministrant of celerity, steam, at our command in every form, to ramble from one extremity of the earth to the other; but the slightest retrospection suffices to

* Though the great Genoese came in sight of St. Salvador, Bahama Islands, on the 11th of October, 1492, it was not until 1497 that he found the continent, the same year that Cabot, the son of a Venetian pilot residing at Bristol, discovered Newfoundland, and named it Prima Vista; the year also (or, as some say, the year before), that Amerigo Vespucci, a Florentine in the service of Spain, and subsequently of Portugal, and again of Spain, reached the east coast, and was fortunate in giving his name to the entire of the continent, north and south. The Bahamas were not known to the English for nearly 200 years (1667) after the discovery by Columbus, when Captain Seyle was nearly wrecked there while proceeding to Carolina, also discovered by Cabot in 1500. The Bahamas were long infested by pirates; but in 1718 Captain Rogers expelled them, and the islands became and have since remained the property of the Crown of England, with the consent of Spain, though the British had had a settlement there long previously.

demonstrate how very different a state of things prevailed at the close of the fifteenth century. The mere existence of a western continent was a phantasy of dream-land, when the mysteries of that mighty waste of waters which separated the then known world from all beyond, was shrouded in obscurity as unfathomable as its deepest depths; when only frail barks and mariners who dreaded to lose sight of the land could be found to attempt the seemingly-desperate fate of exploring an unknown sea in search of what at best existed but in the imagination of those who were regarded as visionaries, and whose presumptuous rashness the very winds themselves seemed to rebuke by blowing with unprecedented constancy in the one direction, as if to proclaim the impossibility of return.* Taking these circumstances into our consideration, a most thrilling interest is attached to this recital that will endure to the latest posterity; and school-boys for generations to come will ponder over the amazing achievements of these wondrous knights-errant of the main with the same eager curiosity as the grown men of to-day.

On the other hand, it must be as readily conceded that there is something painfully oppressive in the records of ancient history, with its never-ending conflict between nations for the aggrandisement of a few ambitious monarchs or republican leaders, in which the destruction of cities, towns, and countries, as well as of the lives of their inhabitants, is the theme perpetually dwelt upon, as if the annihilation of his kind were the only achievement entitling man to the admiration of humanity. War in all its horrors, and the military extirpation of our species, is the delight of the classic chroniclers, whether in poetry or

> * He turned, but what strange thoughts perplexed his soul,
> When, lo! no more attracted to the Pole,
> The Compass, faithless to the circling Vane,
> Fluttered and fixed, fluttered and fixed again'
> At length, as by some unseen Hand imprest,
> It sought, with trembling energy, the West!
> 'Ah, no!' he cried, and calmed his anxious brow;
> ' Ill, nor the signs of ill, 'tis Thine to show,
> Thine but to lead me where I wished to go!'
>   ROGERS' COLUMBUS.

prose; and its accompaniments of battles, sieges, pillage, murder, and atrocities such as nature revolts at, are depicted with a species of barbaric satisfaction, calculated (as it no doubt often did) to evoke the vengeance of the Deity against enormities perpetrated in the mere wantonness of licentious ferocity, and too frequently lacking the miserable palliative of provocation. Infinitely is it to be deplored that this sanguinary animus was carried, in a large degree, by the Spaniards and Portuguese, but probably still more by the Dutch (with whom, however, we are not now concerned), into their conquests in the New World; but it brought with it its own retributive punishment; and finally, under Providence, became the most potent instrument that caused war to be looked upon as an enormous evil, and a curse upon any country unrighteously practising it.

To the discovery of the New World we may fairly trace the benign effects of that wholesome correction of a most pernicious estimate of human merit. This, gradually softening the minds of men, instilled the principle of commercial intercourse amongst nations; demonstrating how much more conducive to true greatness and human happiness is the cultivation of amicable relations than even the most successful aggression and devastation, and the acquisition of wealth by iniquitous appliances.

It was in the year 1492 that Columbus landed on one of the West India islands. (See *ante*, page 8.) Subsequently, what is now termed the Spanish Main was crossed in rapid succession by various Peninsular adventurers, one and all of whom were distinguished by bravery the most exalted and selfishness the most abased, each attribute being inflamed by a fanaticism that sought to honour God and appease His anger towards their iniquities, by incredible offences in the name of religion against the unoffending aborigines. Preëminent, perhaps, among these bold bad captains, on the score of political prescience, military skill, and administrative civil ability, as well as from the magnitude of his acquisitions, was Hernan Cortez, who, in 1521, conquered the table land of Mexico, its coasts being discovered some three

12 INTRODUCTION.

years before.* The immensity and enormity of his massacres, and the perfidy that distinguished them—the ingenuity of his multitudinous outrages upon the Emperor Montezuma and scores

* Though his scope embraces no part of the West Coast, nor any portion of the East Coast beyond the line, the author hopes, by the introduction of a few of the more prominent facts connected with each republic, to render this volume somewhat useful to those of his readers who may be desirous of a slight *précis* of the history and position of the various states of South America, but who would, nevertheless, be deterred from entering upon details of feuds and complications more unintelligibly perplexing than the records of the dynastic chaos of the Saxon heptarchy, or the septic entanglements of the earliest Celtic kings. To this end, therefore, there will be appended a note on each of the outlying districts, if we may so call them, as they occur in the text; and first in the foregoing order comes

MEXICO.—After the usual experience of viceregal misrule, common to all the Spanish transmarine dependencies, this noble province threw off the yoke and asserted its independence in 1820, and virtually achieved it about a year afterwards, principally through Iturbide, a Spanish soldier of great valour and military skill, and who might probably have done for the land of his adoption what Washington had effected for the United States. Unlike that great character, however, he abused for his own selfishness the power he acquired: and, not content with being head of the state as regent on behalf of the people, he perfidiously caused himself to be proclaimed emperor, in 1822, and imperial revenues and honours to be decreed to himself and to his family. These measures, with many others of a like kind, produced such general defection, that he assembled the dispersed members of Congress in the capital, in 1823, and abdicated, agreeing to reside for the remainder of his life in Italy, on which condition a large allowance was made him. But, faithless to his word in this instance, as before, he returned from Leghorn, through England, attempted a revolution, miserably failed in raising any followers, and was ignominiously shot, at Padilla, in Santander, by La Garza, commander of that province, pursuant to instructions from the provincial legislature, in 1824. Vittoria, one of the ablest lieutenants of Iturbide in the war of independence, had been proclaimed president the year before, and the year after ('25) a treaty of commerce was ratified with Great Britain. Such proceedings, with the recognition that was soon to follow of the independence of the revolted country, had formed a topic of urgent interest at the Congress of Verona, in 1822, when, seeing what was looming in the future of South America, the Duke of Wellington, plenipotentiary from England, instructed by Mr Canning, in continuation of the policy of Lord Castlereagh, to whom the Duke had just succeeded, presented a note, stating, that 'The connection subsisting between the subjects of his Britanic Majesty and the other parts of the globe has for long rendered it necessary for him to recognise the existence, *de facto*, of governments formed in different places, so far as was necessary to conclude treaties with them. The relaxation of the authority of of thousands of his subjects—have rendered his name indelibly detestable, though there were many traits of true heroism about him, beyond what their biographers have been able to preserve

Spain in her colonies of South America has given rise to a host of pirates and adventurers,—an insupportable evil, which it is impossible for England to extirpate without the aid of the local authorities occupying the adjacent coasts and harbours; and the necessity of this cooperation cannot but lead to the recognition, *de facto*, of a number of governments of their own creation.'

Austria, Russia, Prussia, and France (represented by M de Chateaubriand), diplomatically ignored this overture to humiliate their royal brother of Spain by admitting that which they were soon afterwards compelled, for their own sakes, to acquiesce in All the efforts of the successor of Ferdinand and Isabella ignominiously failed to win back or retain any portion of the glorious inheritance of the throne of the Indies A vast expedition, sent against Mexico, surrendered to the now successful revolutionists in 1829, a few months after the expulsion of the Spaniards had been decreed Unfortunately, however, democratic anarchy soon supervened upon monarchic despotism; for hardly was the old tyranny got rid of, than Guerrero, the president, was deposed; and Mexico has since been but another word for whatever is most unwise in foreign policy or most pernicious in domestic administration. In 1838 war was declared against France, and of course, ended in disaster to Mexico, after five months' duration, the most memorable incidents being the capture of the strong fortress of St Jean d'Ulloa, by Prince Joinville, who greatly distinguished himself; and the brave defence of Vera Cruz, by Santa Anna, who there lost a leg. This soldier of fortune, something of the stamp of Rosas, having been repeatedly elected to supreme power, deposed, exiled, imprisoned, and restored, is once more president, with what prospect of continuance it is impossible to tell Neither misfortune, nor experience of the impolicy of excessive severity, seems to have mitigated the innate ferocity of the man's character With a defiance of opinion more in consonance with the era of the Borgias than of constitutional government, or even of a civilized government in the middle of the 19th century, only as late as November last the Dictator caused death to be inflicted, by shooting, without the pretext of a trial, and as though they were the veriest wild beasts, on Senhor Tornel, formerly President Arista's Minister of War, and Senhor de la Rosa, who was minister for foreign affairs immediately after the capitulation of the city of Mexico, and was the immediate instigator of Santa Anna's expulsion from the country on that occasion, being also the writer of the letter officially informing him of his disgrace Their offence was, simply, being obnoxious to the dictator—nothing more Like Rosas, however, he has evinced more consideration for the foreign creditor than might have been expected; and about the period of the barbarity just named, devoted a considerable sum in liquidation of the more pressing of these demands, his ability to do so arising, it was said, (though the authority is as apocryphal as the circumstance itself) from a donation by the pope, as an equivalent for of his invading cotemporary destroyers on the same scene. As was the case, too, with so many of them, his fruit in the end proved but bitterness and ashes; for though the vast enrichment of the revenues of Spain, through his means, extorted from an ungrateful sovereign a marquisate, and the grant of a portion of the territories he had conquered, he died at home, the object

the restoration of the order of the Jesuits in Mexico. Others say that his funds have accrued from a sale to the United States of territory adjoining the present Californian possessions of the Union; and that, with the proceeds, he means to repeat Iturbide's experiment in imperial power and title. Be this as it may, the area of Santa Anna's sway, is much less now than it was formerly; for, owing to a succession of decisive repulses sustained from the United States, with which war was declared in 1846, and carried on till the beginning of 1848, Mexico has lost California; Texas having been annexed to the States in 1846; Yucatan, &c, having also seceded; and now, of the once prodigious territory of the Montezumas, and known in Spanish colonial history as the viceroyalty of Mexico, there remains, according to the treaty of 1848, but the comparatively narrow strip of land between the Gulf of Mexico and the Pacific.

This, though only a fragment of what it once belonged to, is still most rich in minerals, and most fruitful in valuable products, and highly important from its position; but nearly all its natural advantages are destroyed by the insecurity and deficiencies of its political institutions, and the incapacity and selfishness of those administering them among a very numerous population, equal, at least, to that of Scotland, after all the curtailments we have spoken of. It is needless to acquaint any reader of the public journals, to whom the words 'Mexican Bondholders' must be a 'horrid, hideous sound of woe, sadder than owl-songs on the midnight blast,' that the finances of the state are in a condition the reverse of consolatory to creditors. For the precise nature of those obligations, in whose fulfilment England is so much interested, we must refer to the very numerous pamphlets published by the various committees appointed in London to advise upon this intricate and unsatisfactory subject. That there is every desire on Santa Anna's part to meet English liabilities, there can be no doubt; one motive for his anxiety being, it is said, the achievement of a stock-jobbing *coup* on his own account, or, rather, on account of the adventurers he is surrounded by. If internal peace could only be secured, the vast resources of the country, and its unparagoned geographical position, midway, as it were, in the very path of the commerce of both hemispheres, would soon permit of its financial difficulties being adjusted. The question is, whether Santa Anna, in putting down anarchy—if he can keep it down—will not commit excesses as bad as the revolutionists in an opposite direction? The latter is the tendency of his acts at the present; but it is impossible to predicate of such a country what may or may not turn up from one hour to another. The representative of Mexico, hitherto charged, until lately, with the difficult task of negociating in this of courtly suspicion and distrust; stung to death by mortification, that all his achievements had been productive of coldness and neglect; where he had most expected to meet with eulogium and honour, he found, like Columbus, (says the eloquent historian of his conquests) that it was possible to deserve too greatly.*

country with the English creditors, has been Colonel Facio. The Mexican diplomatic staff in London consists of Senhor de Castillo y Lanzas, 10, Park-place, Regent's-park, envoy extraordinary and minister plenipotentiary; Don Augustin A. Franco, first secretary; Don Jose Hidalgo, 2nd secretary; Don Ignacio Luijano, attaché; Don B. G. Farias, 32, Great Winchester-street, vice-consul.

Though Consuls were sent, for commercial purposes, to nearly all the important ports of the new South American states, as early as October, 1823, it was not for several years afterwards that political or diplomatic representatives were despatched. The first was Mr Alexander Cockburn, as envoy extraordinary and minister plenipotentiary to Columbia, February, 1826; second, Sir R. Ker Porter, chargé d'affaires to Venezuela, July, 1835; third, Mr Turner, envoy extraordinary and minister plenipotentiary to New Granada, June, 1837; and fourth, Mr W. Wilson, chargé d'affaires to Bolivia, 1837. These states will be severally noticed as they occur in the text. It was in March, 1835, that Sir Richard Pakenham, now British Minister in Portugal [see Lisbon] was accredited as plenipotentiary to Mexico. At present the same post is filled by Mr Percy William Doyle (many years chargé d'affaires there) whose salary is £3,600, with £400 a-year house rent; secretary of legation, William Edward Thornton, salary, £600, paid attaché, Mr A. H. Hastings Berkeley, salary, £200; and an unpaid attaché. The annexed list exhibits the names and salaries of the British consular corps in Mexico:—Mexico, F. Glennie, consul, £400; Vera Cruz, F. Giffard, consul, £500; Tampico, consul, Cleland Cumberlege, £500; San Blas, Eustace W. Barron, consul, £300; Mazatlan, S. Thomson, vice-consul, £150; Acapulco, Charles Wilthew, consul, £400.

* In the month of February, 1554, he addressed a long letter to the emperor,—it was the last he ever wrote him,—soliciting his attention to his suit. He begins, by proudly alluding to his past services to the Crown. 'He had hoped, that the toils of youth would have secured him repose in his old age. For forty years he had passed his life with little sleep, bad food, and with his arms constantly by his side. He had freely exposed his person to peril, and spent his substance in exploring distant and unknown regions, that he might spread abroad the name of his sovereign, and bring under his sceptre many great and powerful nations. All this he had done, not only without assistance from home, but in the face of obstacles thrown in his way by rivals and by enemies, who thirsted like leeches for his blood. He was now old, infirm, and embarrassed with debt. Better had it been for him not to have known the liberal intentions of the emperor, as intimated by his grants, since he should then have devoted himself to the care of his estates, and not have been compelled, as he now was, to contend with the officers of the Crown, against whom it was more difficult to defend himself than to win the land from the enemy.' He concludes with beseeching his sovereign to 'order the Council of the Indies, with the other tribunals which had cognisance of his suits, to come to a decision;

Passing next to him before whose golden sun the star of Cortez waned, we find that the ruthless valour and iron perseverance of Pizarro subjugated Peru* in 1531, while one of his

since he was too old to wander about like a vagrant, but ought, rather, during the brief remainder of his life, to stay at home and settle his account with Heaven, occupied with the concerns of his soul, rather than with his substance.' This appeal to his sovereign, which has something in it touching from a man of the haughty spirit of Cortez, had not the effect to quicken the determination of his suit. He still lingered at the court, from week to week, and from month to month, beguiled by the deceitful hopes of the litigant, tasting all that bitterness of the soul which arises from hope deferred. After three years more, passed in this unprofitable and humiliating occupation, he resolved to leave his ungrateful country and return to Mexico. He had proceeded as far as Seville, accompanied by his son, when he fell ill of an indigestion, caused, probably, by irritation and trouble of mind. This terminated in dysentery, and his strength sank so rapidly under the disease, that it was apparent his mortal career was drawing towards its close.—
Prescott

* PERU.—Referring to what has been already said as regards Mexico for a general notion of the relationship between Spain and her colonies, when the spirit of revolt began to develope itself in the latter, it is only necessary to add here that, since its emancipation, Peru has, like all the congeries of republics of which it forms one, been a prey to civil dissension and military turmoil. Of late years its increasing commerce, the vast pecuniary means it has discovered, in its guano islands, of meeting its engagements with the European creditor, and the comparatively pacific spirit that prevails in its councils and in those of the neighbouring states, are producing their natural results; and, despite occasional exceptions, there is every reason to look for a prosperous future. The conquest of Peru having been effected with infinitely more ease than that of Mexico, as far as the mere military resistance of the natives was concerned, it continued for nearly 300 years subject to Spain, and formed its last stronghold in that quarter of the world. The history of the struggles for independence, from the time that the first Protector, San Martin, [see Chili, page 18] entered the country with the combined Chilian and Buenos Ayrean army, and proclaimed its freedom at Lima, the capital, in 1821, till the Spaniards were finally expelled, would embrace the biography of the commander just named, and the still more celebrated one, Bolivar, who, with his victorious troops from Columbia, to which he had given liberty in 1821, mainly contributed to the liberation of Peru, whereof he became President in 1825, San Martin retiring in 1822, with these memorable words:—' I have proclaimed the independence of Chili and Peru; I have taken the standard with which Pizarro came to enslave the empire of the Incas; and I have ceased to be a public man.' Bolivar ran through pretty much the same vicissitudes of popular caprice as we have recounted in the case of Santa Anna, though an incomparably superior character in every respect; and, after numberless feuds, and escaping plots against his life by those he had raised to power, was on the point of returning from voluntary seclusion, on his patrimonial estate, to assume once more the direction of affairs, in obedience to the voice of the public, who, too late, found out that he was the only man for the occasion,

followers, who most resembled him in the cruelty of his life, as he did in the untimeliness of his death (caused by a quarrel with his old master about the spoil), after the seeming consum-

when he died in 1830, in his 47th year, leaving behind the highest reputation which South American history has afforded, not only as a commander and an administrator, but as a constitutional legislator. Repeated revolutions have since ensued, partly caused by rivalries of internal factions, and partly by the hostilities of neighbouring states, which, being themselves torn with dissension, and constantly changing their territorial status, have rendered war upon Peru, or on the part of Peru, almost unavoidable. This is the case at present; Bolivia, under its President, Belzu, having invaded Peru, and protracted hostilities being certain. Under such circumstances it is hardly necessary to add, that the finances of the country have been inadequate to its expenditure, and that, consequently, the foreign creditors have fared exceedingly ill. Of late, however, the prospects have greatly improved, owing to the immense demand for that peculiar manure which is found in the condition most approved by agriculturists on the Peruvian coast, and in the next greatest perfection on the neighbouring coast of Chili, whence, indeed, the first cargo, which created so much interest, was brought a few years back into Liverpool, causing small observation, however, for a long time. But, unluckily for the foreign creditor and the true interests of the Peruvian government, the latter fixed so high a price on the commodity, as to create a complete monopoly, attended with most of the mischiefs of which all monopolies are the parents. Until the close of the last year, it was imagined that the supply of this most essential ingredient in farming economy was literally inexhaustible, and that the cost to the consumer might be kept up at the original excessive rate. About that period, however, it was ascertained, through a survey instituted by Admiral Moresby, commanding the British squadron on the West Coast, that at the then rate of demand (and it has gone on increasing since) the whole stock (many millions of tons though it was) would be exhausted in the course of about twenty years. Moreover, as the discovery, first, of the unique virtues of guano, and, secondly, of its deposit in the finest known quality and greatest quantity here, were purely accidental, it is not improbable, indeed is regarded as certain, that there will also be discoveries of other excellent fertilizers of a like kind, and of other vast deposits of guano, if not quite so excellent, yet sufficiently so to deprive Peru of its principal customers at existing rates. Should either of these occurrences take place—should it be found, as Lord Clarendon anticipated, in answer to a deputation on the subject, that nitrate of soda is extractable from the immense heaps of fish refuse on the Newfoundland coast, and will supply, as chemists believe, the fructifying element of guano; or should it be found that those deposits of guano in more damp latitudes, —the Falklands, for instance—will admit of being profitably freed from the effects of moisture, of course the value of the Peruvian commodity will decline accordingly, and so will the prospects of the bondholders, who have mation of his ambition — Diego Almagro — having committed horrors till then almost unheard of, over-ran Chili* in 1535.

probably been amongst the greatest of all the sufferers from the *mala fides* and impoverishment of South American debtors. A species of new bonds have recently been created, to the great detriment of the interest of the holders of the old ones, and the dissatisfaction is extreme, especially as the government, instead of being warned by the facts we have recounted in respect to guano, and by the discovery of valuable guano islands by North American citizens in the Carribean Sea, have actually advanced the price of the commodity to the extent of the recently enhanced freights, as compared with the usual rates of shipping charges.

Apart from the monetary, the diplomatic credit of Peru has always been respectably sustained at the Court of St. James's. The corps at present consists of Don Manuel de Mendiburu, minister plenipotentiary, Don Francisco de Rivero, consul-general, 78, Grosvenor-street, Grosvenor-square, Don Emilio Altheus, D. M. Espantosa, and Major D. S. Osma, attachés. Consul's-office, 6, Copthall-court. Consuls—J. E. Naylor, Liverpool; R. J. Todd, Cardiff; John G. Dodd, Newcastle-upon-Tyne; Edward Wright, Dublin.

England is represented in Peru by Mr. S. H. Sullivan, chargé d'affaires at Lima, salary as such £1,700 a-year, besides the usual £1 per diem allowed to all functionaries of that class discharging consular duties. Until last year (1853) the diplomatic salary was £2,000. At Callao, the port of Lima, the salary of the consul (Mr. J. Barton) has also been reduced from £500 to £200, but the fees of office still make the post very lucrative. At Islay, the vice-consul, Mr. T. Crompton, receives £500; and at Arica and Payta, Mr. G. H. Nugent and Mr. Alexander Blacker, vice-consuls, £300 and £100 respectively.

* CHILI.—Though probably none of the Spanish conquests in South America were effected with greater ease than that of Chili—a sort of dependency on the Incas of Peru, and faithful to their cause long after it was lost at head-quarters—nowhere were the natives impressed so much at first with the superiority of the invincible stranger, a sum equivalent to half a million of ducats being presented to Almagro, in recognition of his 'divinity' when he crossed the Cordilleras; yet none of their acquisitions, subsequently cost the conquerors more trouble. Notwithstanding the scandalous cruelties of the invaders, it was not till 1546, ten years after Valdivia (a second lieutenant of Pizarro's) had entered their country, that resistance was wholly put down. The Chilians, the last in being subdued, were also among the first to take advantage of the troubles of the mother country in her decrepitude and decline. On the invasion of Spain by the French, and the rout of the Spanish Bourbons in 1809, Chili, affecting to be solicitous for the sovereignty of Ferdinand VII., and to be desirous of administering the government of itself in his name, established a junta in the capital, St. Jago, in 1810, and ultimately avowed itself a decided separatist. Spain, however, was still able to make head against the revolutionists; and after a series of encounters, in

He exterminated the family of Atahualpa, the last of the Incas, in a mode which only the most hardened familiars of the Inquisition, in the mother country, could read of without emotion, and to this day the records of such revolting transactions constitute probably the foulest blot on the Columbian escutcheon of the country of Du Guesclin and the Cid. But the sins of these men may be said to have been avenged by heaven in the noon of their iniquities. Pizarro, having defeated Almagro at Cuzco,

which fortune alternated rapidly, she vindicated her authority by a very decisive victory at Rancagua, in 1817. This, however, did not prevent the popular party triumphing at Chacabuco, in the same year, and seizing on the capital. Again the king's troops succeeded at Chancarayada, but, once more, and conclusively, the republicans carried all before them in the eventful battle of Maypu, in 1818, though it was not till the beginning of 1826 that the province was finally freed from the presence of the peninsular cohorts, and declared independent, the old country itself, however, refusing any such recognition till 1842, when a treaty of peace and friendship was signed at Madrid, and ratifications exchanged in 1845. Throughout these wars the most conspicuous revolutionary leader was General San Martin, a soldier of Irish origin, as his name imports,* being one of the many of his countrymen whom the struggles for independence brought forward in the Spanish colonies, in none more so than in Chili, the first Supreme Director, as the officer elected by the juntas was originally called, being Barnardo O'Higgins, with whom were associated Col. O'Leary, General Miller, and numerous others 'racy of the soil' of saints and shillelaghs. Of all the European celebrities, however, who figured on the stage of South American strife, none are to be compared to the heroic Lord Cochrane, now the venerable Admiral Earl Dundonald, who, having fitted out a ship of his own in England in the cause of the patriots, and being appointed to the command of the Chilian fleet, co-operating with the land forces of Bolivar, displayed that characteristic skill and enterprise which have so preeminently distinguished him throughout his

---

* His aid-de-camp was General John O'Brien, afterwards accredited by the Banda Oriental, or State of the Uruguay, as diplomatic representative to England, where he contributed greatly to familiarise the British public with the bearings of the Plate Question, and to popularise the cause of Monte Videan resistance to the aggression of Rosas. In this object he was essentially assisted by his learned and accomplished countryman, Mr W Bernard Macabe, a distinguished London journalist, and well-known author in historical and miscellaneous literature, who discharged the duties of acting consul-general for the Uruguay in London for some years, till the end of 1852, when he proceeded to Dublin, where he has since prosecuted his intellectual avocations with his customary assiduity and success. The General, we believe, is now residing in honoured retirement, in his old age, in the neighbourhood of Valparaiso, on a property allowed him by the Government of Chili, to whose original independence his exertions materially contributed.

and put many of his officers to death, in cold blood, had his old comrade strangled and then beheaded in Lima, where the despot himself was assassinated by young Almagro, who, in his turn, being defeated in battle, also at Cuzco, by Vaca de Castro, was likewise put to death by decapitation

Passing next to the Portuguese discoveries, that of Brazil was effected by Alvarez de Cabral, he having landed, by accident, through stress of weather, at Porto Seguro, on the 24th of April, 1500, calling the country Santa Cruz (Holy Cross) in gratitude for his delivery from shipwreck, but the appellation was afterwards altered to that which it at present bears, signifying redwood, the well-known substance familiar to us as Brazil wood; yet it was the subsequent exploration of this coast, some four years afterwards, that enabled Amerigo Vespucci to eternise his own name as the accepted discoverer of the continent itself.

chivalrous and romantic career, some few incidents of which will be found mentioned in our notice of a congenial and no less heroic spirit, Admiral Grenfell, of the Brazilian service, in which Dundonald played a conspicuous part

From what we have said already, both of Mexico and also of Peru, it will naturally be inferred that Chili has suffered greatly from internal disorders; but, unlike those countries, she has contrived to avoid a very onerous national debt, and consequently her credit abroad is comparatively very good, indeed, better probably than that of any South American state, save Brazil, whose securities rank next to those of Great Britain itself The recent gold discoveries in California and Australia have immensely increased her export trade, and will continue to do so for an indefinite period, while a large source of domestic revenue has been opened up by the possession of guano islands (of which more hereafter), second only in extent, and scarcely second in richness, to those treasures of a like kind whereof we have spoken under the head of Peru, the example of which country is followed as to the maintenance of the price of the article at an exorbitant rate

The Chilian diplomatic and consular corps in England consists of Spencer N. Dickson, consul, 8, Great Winchester-street, London; W W Alexander, consul, Bristol, Cardiff, and Newport, William Jackson, consul, Liverpool; Thomas W Fox, jun, consul, Plymouth; James H Wolff, consul, Southampton; John W Leach, consul, Swansea The British diplomatic and consular corps in Chili consists of the Hon E J. Harris, chargé d'affaires at the capital, St Jago, salary £1,600, and the usual consular allowance of £1 per diem, consul at Valparaiso, Mr Henry Rouse, salary £300, reduced from £700; consul at Coquimbo, Mr David Ross, salary £300; and vice-consul at Conception, Mr Robert Cunningham, salary £250—all exclusive of fees

Another instance of the vagaries and mutations of geographical nomenclature, in this region of the world, occurs in connection with the great achievement that next solicits our notice, viz, the doubling of the Cape, and consequent opening-up of an oceanic highway to India. This was second in importance only to the discovery of the New World itself, and, indeed, well nigh placed Portugal on a par with Spain in honorary maritime status. Vasco de Gama, whose exploits inspired the muse of Camoens in the Lusiad,* which noble poem is in a great measure only a rythmetical narrative of the perils of the navigator, 'made the Cape' November 20th, 1497; and, with the expressiveness of all the earlier mariners, named it the 'Cape of Tempests,'† and it was afterwards known as the 'Lion of the Sea,' and the 'Head of

---

* The subject of this poem is the establishment of the Portuguese empire in India, but whatever of chivalrous, great, beautiful, or noble, could be gathered from the traditions of his country, has been interwoven into the story. Among all the heroic poets, says Schlegel, either of ancient or modern times, there has never, since Homer, been any one so intensely national, or so loved or honoured by his countrymen, as Camoens. It seems as if the national feelings of the Portuguese had centred and reposed themselves in the person of this poet, whom they consider as worthy to supply the place of a whole host of poets, and as being in himself a complete literature to his country. Of Camoens they say,

> Vertere fas, æquare nefas, æquabilis uni
> Est sibi, par nemo, nemo secundus erit

Few modern poems in any language, have been so frequently translated as the 'Lusiad.' Mr Adamson, whose 'Memoirs of the Life and Writings of Camoens' must be familiar to the reader, notices one Hebrew translation of it, five Latin, six Spanish, four Italian, three French, four German, and two English. Of the two English versions one is that of Sir R. Fanshawe, written during Cromwell's usurpation, and distinguished for its fidelity to the original, the other is that of Mickle, who, unlike the former, took great liberties with the original, but whose additions and alterations have met with great approbation from all critics—except, as indeed was to be expected, from the Portuguese themselves.—*Dr Cauvin*.—In the course of the present year (1854) another English version, from the pen of Sir Thomas Mitchell, Surveyor-General of New South Wales, and formerly on the staff in the Peninsula, has been issued by Messrs Boone, of Bond-street, in one volume, with an engraving, said to be an excellent likeness, of the poet.

† 'Eu sou aquelle occulto, e grande Cabo,
A quem chamais vos outros Tormentario,
Que nunca a Ptolemeo, Pomponio, Estrabo,
Plinio, e quantos passaram, foi notorio.
Aqui toda a Africana Costa acabo
Neste meu nunca visto promontorio,
Que para o polo Antartico se estende,
A quem vossa ousadia tanto offende'

CAMOENS, canto 5, verse 50

Africa.' These designations were different indeed to that it has long rejoiced in—the 'Cape of Good Hope'—so called by John the Second of Portugal, who drew a favourable augury of future discoveries thence, because of his adventurous subject, Diaz, having reached the extremity of Africa, at that point, though in doing so, he perished there in 1500, having divided with Gama the honour of being its original discoverer, and supposed by some to have preceded him by nearly ten years. Previous, however, to this latter occurrence, even if we accept the earliest date claimed for Diaz, mankind was amazed by reports of the circumnavigation of the globe—a feat, which, like those already named, has been a fruitful source of controversy as to the just recipient of the meed of priority. Sebastian de Elcano is, perhaps, the most generally accepted by foreign writers. Goralva and Alvalradi, both Spaniards, performed the task—astounding, indeed, when we think of the fragile craft employed, and the unknown courses ventured upon—in one and the same year, 1537, without concert with each other. Mendana, another Spaniard, repeated it in 1567—preceding our own immortal sovereign of the seas, Drake, by ten years. But long anterior to all these, was the Portuguese Magellan, who, in 1519, being in the service of Spain, determined the sphericity of the earth by keeping a westerly course through the straits bearing his name, across the Pacific, and returning to the spot he set out from, or rather the ship did, for he was killed at the Philippines, on his passage back, the whole voyage occupying three years

> ' In me the spirit of the Cape behold,
> That Rock by you the Cape of Torments named,
> By Neptune's rage in horrid Earthquake framed,
> Where Jove's red bolts o'er Titan's offspring flamed
> With wide-stretch'd piles I guard the pathless strand,
> And Afric's southern mound unmoved I stand;
> Nor Roman prow, nor daring Tyrian oar,
> 'Ere dashed the white wave foaming to my shore,
> Nor Greece, nor Carthage, ever spread the sail
> On these my seas to catch the trading gale
> You, you alone, have dared to plough my main,
> And with the human voice disturb my lonesome reign '
>   Mickle's Translation of this verse, the 'Lusiad,' p. 205

INTRODUCTION 23

and twenty-nine days.* These, and a series of marvels, only subordinate in wonder because inferior in importance, kept the western world in unflagging excitement for a long succession of

* STEAM THROUGH THE STRAITS OF MAGELLAN TO THE PACIFIC.—In a work like this, almost specially devoted to an exemplification of the achievements and the prospects of steam enterprise in South America, we take the earliest opportunity of placing on record the efforts of a gentleman, who, in those distant waters first explored by Magellan, and through the very straits named after that daring navigator, conducted a steamer to the West Coast long before the Royal Mail Company, as mentioned in our prefatory remarks, sent any of their paddle-wheels to the East Coast. The first steamers that ever navigated these straits were the Peru and Chili, belonging to the Pacific Steam Navigation Company, under the orders of Captain George Peacock, a gentleman well known in connection with naval steam tactics, now superintendent of the Southampton docks, and vice-consul for the Uruguay at that port. Leaving England in command of the Peru, in July, 1840, and touching only at Rio de Janeiro for a supply of fuel, he anchored in Port Famine, Patagonia, on the 13th of September, after a passage at sea of only 43 days. These vessels, built by Messrs Curling and Young, of Limehouse, were contracted and fitted out with great care, under the superintendence of Captain Peacock, being also rigged on a new plan proposed by him, whereby they were enabled to proceed under sail alone during a great part of the voyage, the steam only having been used for 21 out of the 43 days occupied between Plymouth and Port Famine. This was an unprecedented feat in the annals of steam navigation up to that period, and has scarcely been surpassed since, as these vessels carried out a large amount of general cargo to Valparaiso, besides their spare machinery, and a great quantity of stores, proving the importance of all steamships for long voyages, whether screw or paddle-wheel, being fully and properly rigged. The Pacific Steam Navigation Company was projected in 1833 by William Wheelwright, Esq., an enterprising American gentleman, who had passed many years on the West Coast of South America, and who obtained exclusive privileges, from the Chilian and Peruvian governments, for establishing steam in the Pacific, provided steamers were placed on the coast within a given period. On Mr Wheelwright's arrival in England he found great difficulty in forming a company, although no one doubted but that the navigation and requirements of the West Coast were, perhaps, better adapted for steam navigation than any other spot on the face of the globe. Unfortunately for the projector, the extreme pressure of the money-market at that time, coupled with the distance of the intended scene of operations, the want of confidence in the grants of South American states, and the political changes to which they were exposed, all conduced to impede the enterprise; and, after passing upwards of three years of untiring patience and suffering, numberless anxieties, heart-sickening vexations, and even personal privations (the fate of too many enterprising men in the prosecution of new and useful projects), and when his capital was nigh

INTRODUCTION.

years, during which Europe tingled with the tidings of vast countries being discovered, assailed, and captured, by mere handfuls of obscure fortune-hunters, and yielding up such exhaustless

wrecked, and his favourite scheme about to be abandoned as hopeless, he had the good fortune to meet with the late Lord Abinger, who, together with the noble members of the Scarlett family, warmly espoused the undertaking, and with the aid of other kind friends, the company was at length formed, and, towards the close of the year 1839, two vessels, of 750 tons and 180 horse power each, were contracted for. The keels were laid Jan., 1840, and the ships built, launched, fitted out, and sent to sea in July, within a period of seven months, no expense being spared to effect this object, with a view of saving the privileges to be conceded by the Chilian government.

This proved to be impracticable, notwithstanding the extraordinary exertions that had been made, owing to the vexatious annoyances of the port authorities at Rio de Janeiro, who exacted such stringent regulations and created such difficulties, that the steamers were delayed fourteen days, where 48 hours would have sufficed. The fine harbour of Port Stanley, at the Falkland Islands, was not then known to possess the facilities it now does for such repairs, nor were there at the time the necessary means of effecting them, otherwise Captain Peacock, who has the highest opinion of that harbour, and has urged it as a port of call and for coaling on the captains of all sailing or steam-vessels coming home from Australia by Cape Horn, would have at once resorted to it, and so saved the almost ruinous delay and vast expense occasioned him at Rio. The consequence of this detention was, that the vessels did not arrive at Port Famine, the southern-most harbour claimed by the republic of Chili, until the 13th of September, whilst the privileges, already alluded to, expired on the first of that month.

By the 18th of September both ships were completed with wood and water, every man, from the captain downwards, assisting in sawing and splitting up drift-wood, found in abundance along the shores of the harbour, an American axe having been provided for each person on board, together with cross-cut saws and iron wedges, for such object, before leaving England. This day, being the 'diesiocho,' or great anniversary of the Chilian Independence, Captain Peacock caused a beacon, 30 feet high, with a large diamond-shaped head, to be erected on the heights of Santa Anna, the western point of the entrance, and, hoisting the Chilian flag upon it at noon, saluted the same from the guns of both ships, accompanied by three hearty British cheers; and having buried a parchment manuscript at the foot of the beacon, in a sealed jar, descriptive of this event and the particulars of the voyage, &c., together with a few new coins of the year 1840, the steamers proceeded into the Pacific, accomplishing the passage from ocean to ocean, a distance of 300 miles, in 30 hours' steaming. Four years subsequently, the Chilian government sent a vessel of war, and took formal possession of this harbour, for a convict establishment, naming it Port Bulnes, after the President at that time in power, when a fort was built round the before mentioned beacon, the jar was dug up, treasures as rendered the Spanish and Portuguese peninsula, for a prolonged season, the richest kingdoms in the world—the veritable 'envy and admiration of surrounding nations.' To all this we may add that momentum given to commerce and navigation which has gone rolling on, until fleets of all nations cover the seas ; and, so far as we are aware at present, not an island now unknown, of any importance, remains to reward the search of him* who has been last commissioned to find one if he can, even in the comparatively

and the manuscript, &c , taken to St Jago, the capital, and there lodged in the government archives. Upon the arrival of the steamers at Valparaiso, by a representation to the government, the privileges of the company were immediately renewed for a period of ten years ; and probably nothing has contributed so much to the advancement, welfare, and prosperity of the Chilian and Peruvian republics, as the successful establishment of steam navigation upon this coast, where the names of Don Guilliermo Wheelwright and Don Jorje Peacock, will perhaps never be forgotten, as they certainly ought not to be The Chilian government, in the course of last year, (1853) renewed its relations with the Pacific Company for continuing steam communication with England, through the Straits, and also for extending steam intercourse to other parts of Europe, in connection with the vessels now rounding the Horn, granting liberal subsidies for that purpose See end of chapter on Amazon

* Captain Denham, R N , who has been sent on an exploratory cruise in the various Archipelagoes of the Southern Pacific, in hope of meeting with an eligible depot for convicts, whom the cessation of transportation to Australia (or at least to all except the Western portion) has thrown on the hands of the home government, very much to the embarrassment of the executive, and to the consternation of the community ; for, as was foreseen when the project was first mooted, not only do the British public dread the introduction among them of the class known in France as *libres forçats*, but the former honest associates of these domesticated 'emancipatists,' to use an antipodean phrase, will not consort with them , hasten to denounce them to their employers as 'black sheep ;' forcibly drive them from amongst them ; and, in fact, surround them with such annoyances that their existence becomes intolerable in the society of any but those who are qualifying for, or have already graduated at, the hulks. The consideration of this subject will be found pursued at some length in treating of the Falklands These islands are in every way admirably adapted, both to meet the difficulties just mooted, as to the disposal of our felonrie, and to supersede the labour of Capt. Denham, should he even be successful in discovering a spot in the southern hemisphere that is not open to innumerable objections on the score—1st, of propinquity to other islands ; 2nd, being at double the distance of the Falklands from the mother country ; and 3rd, the cost of conveyance being proportionably great ; saying nothing of the expensiveness of founding a new settlement in a place that is already deserted, or from which the aborigines, if any, must be removed.

little frequented Polynesian group, for the penal purposes of England.

I will not dwell on the different results that have attended different courses of action with reference to the conquered territories of North and South America; nor attempt to trace the decline of one power at the expense of another. Spain and Portugal, unfortunately for themselves, dealt with their gifts on purely selfish principles; and the consequence of such a system was, not only the loss of the greater part of their colonies, but an almost total estrangement between the parent and child, never afterwards thoroughly healed. We attempted the same game in North America, and the giant-like progress of the United States has followed; only that, wiser in our generation, more forgiving, and actuated by true commercial principles, we have cultivated, to the utmost extent, relations of amity and good-will with the new power, and both countries are largely gainers thereby, and will continue to be so while the same feelings of mutual concession and respect actuate both.

Whilst, therefore, North America has made such astonishing progress, and completely outstrips the Old World in rapidity of thought and execution, carrying her commerce and people to the limits of the habitable globe, the states to the southward have had many severe ordeals to go through—arising, in the first place, from the cause just mentioned, viz., that the mother countries considered their colonies as mere appanages, and prevented communication, in some cases even intercourse, with other nations. Secondly, from the disseverment of the link which united them to Europe, having an entirely new phase to pass through. new forms of government to establish, and fresh relations to cultivate; whilst another immediate effect of the revolution was to drive away most of the wealthy inhabitants who, being Spanish and Portuguese citizens, were not a little vain of their superiority in that respect to their colonial-born brethren. This fruitful source of dissent and violence in nearly all the disturbances by which the several states were torn is by no means wholly obliterated to this day, any more than in some of the transmarine possessions of Great Britain, in either hemisphere. Then came intestine divisions among the American-born colonists themselves, raging between the upstart leaders of mushroom parties, whose very names it taxed the memory of men at the time to remember; and, as a matter of course, there followed all the thousand drawbacks resulting from a state of anarchic confusion. Hence, as is obvious must have been the case under such circumstances, material progress has been slow, and political progress for a long time almost imperceptible, if not frequently retrogressive, if one may use a phrase so seemingly contradictory. Moreover, until of late years very little was known of the internal resources of South America, with the exception of the Brazils—a country to which a variety of circumstances conspired to impart an impetus along the groove of civilization and consequent advancement. Paramount amongst those aids was undoubtedly the establishment there, in 1806, of the old Portuguese monarchy, consequent upon the European troubles of the house of Braganza. The inappreciable advantage of this regular form of government, arising out of local monarchic institutions, that country has retained, though under a new sovereign and with a liberalized system of administration, ever since, with every guarantee for continuously rapid but enduring improvement. Still, even Brazil was, to Europeans, comparatively speaking, an unknown region, to which, in incongruous confusion, attached associations of the soft and the savage, of barbarism and luxury, of the majestic and the feeble, in the minds of all nearly whose reading about her was not corrected by personal familiarity

ith the country itself. But ignorance so arising is being happily fast dissipated; and it shall not be the author's fault if its departure be not further expedited on some points to which it still adheres.

Both the Spaniards and Portuguese possess works of rare merit, far exceeding in magnitude and minuteness any we can boast of, illustrating the achievements of their early navigators, and the rise and progress of their former colonial possessions.

But few of these works have been rendered familiar to the British public, and are very imperfectly known, even to those writers who profess to treat of the same or similar subjects. Of course we except Prescott, the appreciation of whose invaluable volumes on the Conquest of Peru, the Conquest of Mexico, and the History of the Reign of Ferdinand and Isabella, is testified by the exhaustion of six large and expensive editions, and one cheaper edition, in this country, besides the incorporation of the fruits of his extraordinary research in a thousand publications that have since been issued on either side of the Atlantic. Previously, however, to Prescott, and in nearly as large a degree, in respect to the territory described, were we indebted to Southey, for his History of Brazil,* to Koster for valuable details of his travels in the northern provinces of the same empire; and to Gardner, for a most elaborate research into its botanical treasures, as also a graphic description of the interior of the empire, which he traversed from north to south.† The hygiene of the same region has been thoroughly investigated, and its rationale expounded with consummate ability and simplicity of style, by my learned and accomplished fellow-townsman, Dr. Dundas, than whom no man was more competent for the task; and I rejoice to see that, though the subject is necessarily of a very circumscribed range, comparatively speaking, and one not very likely to command public

---

* The History of Brazil—his *opus majus*, a work on which he hoped to base the remembrance of his name—now appeared, the most conspicuous and elaborate of his works, and written *con amore* It forms a branch of the more extensive History of Portugal, which he had no leisure to complete. The materials from which this work was constructed had been collected by his uncle, the Rev Herbert Hill, were unrivalled in value, and accessible to him alone No political bias interrupted the straightforwardness and breadth of his judgment, and his poetic fervour found scope in the character of the clime, the productions of the soil, and the features of savage life, which he describes in the most glowing colours —Life of Southey, by Charles T Brown —London: Chapman and Hall 1854

† Travels in the Interior of Brazil; principally through the Northern Provinces and the Gold and Diamond Districts, during the years 1836-41. By the late George Gardner, M D, F L S, Superintendent of the Royal Botanic Gardens, Ceylon —London Reeve and Co 1853.

attention, its treatment was so masterly, that nearly all the professional journals in the kingdom received it as an important contribution to medical literature.* Its perusal, however, may be also recommended to the general reader as containing notices of Brazilian life and manners and scenery nowhere else to be met with, and which the peculiar facilities enjoyed by the author enabled him to describe with a life-like minuteness whose truthfulness at once stamps its accuracy both on the stranger at a distance and on the most experienced Brazilian resident or native. In speaking thus, I am merely echoing well-recognized facts; my opinion, which would of course be utterly valueless in a medical sense, being in no degree warped by the personal obligation Dr. Dundas has placed me under from the circumstance of his having kindly consented to enrich this volume with a special chapter on a theme analogous to that which his 'Sketches' are devoted to.

It is, however, the now patriarchal, or, as he calls himself, 'Antediluvian' Humboldt, who has showered upon European understanding the light of scientific knowledge concerning the vast South American continent, and his inimitable descriptions of the country and its natural resources have scarcely been appreciated amongst us as they deserve. It is only when confronted with the great fact, so long regarded as the sentimental aspiration of utopiaists, that South America is actually becoming an additional field for our industry and enterprise—when its magnificent fluvial highways are about being traversed by an endless succession of steamers, and its plains by railways—that we really discover how infinitesimal is our knowledge of those resources or capabilities to whose development these means can alone effectually conduce. As a medium of forming an estimate of the material position, as

* Sketches of Brazil; including New Views on Tropical and European Fever With Remarks on a Premature Decay of the System, incident to Europeans, on their return from Hot Climates By ROBERT DUNDAS, M.D, Physician to the Northern Hospital, Liverpool; formerly Acting Surgeon to H M 60th Regiment; and for twenty-three years Medical Superintendent of the British Hospital, Bahia 8vo., price 9s —London: John Churchill, Prince's-street, Soho Liverpool: Deighton and Laughton, and Rockliff and Sons

well as of the natural features of the countries described by him. Humboldt cannot be too highly commended, as the author, of all others, whose flowing narrative, profundity of reflection, and copiousness of illustration—commensurate with the greatness of the subject itself—will amply repay all ordinary curiosity; apart from that superabounding erudition and scientific affluence which pervade the whole works of the great living father of historical philosophers, though singularly freed, like the treatises of our own Herschel, from technicalities that repel the uninitiated As relates to the Rio Plata and its immense tributaries, we have had, in the course of the preceding year, Sir W. Parish's elaborate and excellent volume,* whose only, though it is undoubtedly a great drawback, is, that having been written obviously from inspiration of Rosas, and through the sources that personage opened to him for the purpose at Buenos Ayres, events are recorded in a light entirely in conformity with the views of the Dictator, whose whole past policy is upheld, and his intended plans prospectively eulogised in a manner to which subsequent events, and the judgment pronounced upon them, furnish a significant commentary. In harmony with Rosas's principle of representing Buenos Ayres as virtually constituting the whole Argentine Confederation, and himself as the exponent of public opinion and the embodiment of actual power therein, Sir Woodbine almost altogether ignores the existence of Monte Video, and scarcely alludes to such a state as the Banda Oriental. Hence, as regards the latter province and its capital, and all pertaining to them, Sir Woodbine's book is a blank, or something worse—a deficiency which it is one of the objects of the present volume, in some

* Buenos Ayres and the Provinces of the Rio de la Plata. from their Discovery and Conquest by the Spaniards to the Establishment of their Political Independence. With some Account of their Present State, Trade, Debt, etc; an Appendix of Historical and Statistical Documents; and a Description of the Geology and Fossil Monsters of the Pampas. By Sir WOODBINE PARISH, K C H, F R.S, G S, Vice-President of the Royal Geographical Society of London, and many years Chargé-d'affaires of H B M. at Buenos Ayres Second Edition, enlarged, with a New Map and Illustrations —London · John Murray, Albemarle Street. 1852 degree, to supply. Of the condition of some of the interior provinces, likewise, Sir Woodbine, being obliged to take his information, not only at second hand, but through a channel in which every thing was conductive to the one end, that of exalting Rosas, or depreciating his opponents, gives us particulars not merely inaccurate, but leading to conclusions the very reverse of what a true state of the case would warrant. On this head, especially as regards by far the most important of all the interior states—Paraguay—it is hoped that the present volume will be found to contain much new and reliable information. For this, the writer is mainly indebted to notes of observations made on the route to, and during a residence in, Assumption, by parties personally cognizant of the late most successful and important mission sent out by Lord Malmesbury, whose prescience, in foreseeing the right moment—and in selecting the right agent, Sir C Hotham, for urging negociations towards that object—the author had the satisfaction of hearing emphatically panegyrized in all commercial circles—whether native, British, or foreign—in the course of his late visit to South America.

Lastly, Mr M'Cann,* whose previous work on the Plate had evinced great knowledge of the subject, has recorded his later experience of some of the Riverine provinces in a very agreeable and instructive work, partly formed on the model of Sir F. Bond Head's fascinating Rough Rides on the Pampas, and embracing a review of mercantile matters and prospects in those countries. Written with that knowledge of trade which only a mercantile man can be expected to possess, its spirit is so dispassionate as to be quite unique in a critic, on topics which would seem to impart their partizan atmosphere to all who endeavour to detail their position

* Two Thousand Miles' Ride through the Argentine Provinces being an Account of the Natural Products of the Country, and Habits of the People; with a Historical Retrospect of the Rio de la Plata, Monte Video, and Corrientes By WILLIAM MAC CANN, Author of the Present Position of Affairs on the River Plate With Illustrations. In Two Volumes — London: Smith, Elder, and Co, 65, Cornhill. Smith, Taylor, and Co, Bombay 1853

to those at a distance. Neither must I, by any means, omit to mention the labours of another of my townsmen, Mr. Thomas Baines, who, with that mastery of detail and facility of statistic exposition which seem to be an heir-loom in the family of the late estimable member for Leeds, placed in a very lucid light, some years ago, a subject to which it was difficult at the time to draw general attention, and a popular elucidation of which could only be expected from a pen so qualified.

But of all portions of South America, there is one perhaps concerning which our knowledge is most imperfect, and with which it is most essential that it should be extended, because of the rapid extension of both native and European enterprise in that quarter. We especially allude to that district of the vast region watered by the Amazon of which Pará (city) may be considered the *entrepot*. Fortunately, two very admirable volumes have recently been directed to supplying our deficiency on this head.* The obligations due to these sources will be found amply acknowledged in the chapter devoted to a consideration of the subject. Our own text is enriched with matter drawn from original authorities, long resident on the spot, and in every way calculated to supply trustworthy intelligence. From these the reader will draw his own deductions, as our informants, not

* 1 A Narrative of Travels on the Amazon and Rio Negro, with an Account of the Native Tribes, and Observations on the Climate, Geology, and Natural History of the Amazon Valley. By ALFRED R. WALLACE. With a Map and Illustrations.—London: Reeve and Co., Henrietta Street, Covent Garden. 1853. 2. The Amazon, and the Atlantic Slopes of South America. A Series of Letters under the Signature of 'Inca.' By M. F. MAURY. LL.D., Lieut. U.S. Navy, who, under date, Washington City, January, 1853, says 'These Letters were originally published by the National Intelligencer and the Union, of this City. They treat of one of the most important commercial questions of the age: they are eagerly sought after in all parts of the country; and though they have been extensively read, the demand for them in a more permanent shape than that of a newspaper is such that the Publisher has obtained leave of their Author to re-issue them in their present form.' On the recent visit of Professor Silliman to Humboldt, at Berlin, the veteran explorer expressed his great gratification at the progress which enterprise was making throughout South America, especially in the region of the Amazon; and made particular mention of the Professor's countryman, Lieutenant Maury, of whose

encumbering their data with disquisition, have left their facts to speak for themselves.

Notwithstanding the number of publications enumerated as being lately issued upon South America, and not taking into account others published in the United States, still there is a field of immense extent, as yet comparatively unexplored and hidden, which requires to be opened up to view, in order to enable us to form a sufficiently accurate judgment of the character and capabilities of such countries as Brazil and the republics bordering on the river Plate and its affluents. The main design, therefore, towards this end on the part of the writer in revisiting the scenes of his early youth, is to endeavour to present some fresh sources of information; partly derived from his own actual observation, and partly from the experience of others, who, possessing the best opportunities, have converted them to the best use in furtherance of the purpose now sought to be attained—viz., the elimination of what shall serve for a compact but comprehensive *precis* of the general condition of the countries named in the title page, and particularly their commercial status and prospective indications of a mercantile complexion To refresh the memory on such analogous subjects as may prove interesting in connection with these matters, there is appended what it is hoped will prove a mass of desirable information, in the shape of a collection of notes, bringing down incidents to the latest practi-

---

work we are now speaking, and from which we shall draw copiously hereafter In giving the gallant Lieutenant all praise, however, we should not omit to acknowledge how much the reading public of this quarter of the globe are indebted for their previous knowledge of the same region to another countryman of his, whose excellent little volume has lately been re-issued in England in a cheap form, by Murray, viz, A Voyage up the River Amazon, including a Residence at Pará, by W. H. EDWARDS; of which it was justly said that it was a work valuable for the information it gave on this very little known part of the world, and likely to excite many adventurous young men to explore the Amazon, so that going back on the traces of Orellana, and crossing to the Pacific, may probably become, ere long, as familiar to our countrymen as a voyage up the Rhine or the Nile. Mr. Edwards' charming little volume has led to such exploration; and the interesting results will be found in our chapter upon the Amazon, which we are particularly desirous of drawing attention to

D

cable period antecedent to publication. In order to interfere as little as possible with the current of the narrative, in which it has been deemed expedient to convey the accompanying observations, the writer intends offering his memoranda in the shape of a record of his voyage, taking in all points touched upon as they naturally arose in connection with it; and incidentally referring to those authors who have exhibited the greatest acquaintance with the topics embraced.

ARGENTINA—OUTWARD BOUND.

CHAPTER I.

OUTWARD BOUND.—LIVERPOOL TO LISBON.

The Argentina on her maiden voyage.—Capacity and capability of the river boat at sea.—From the Mersey to the Tagus in four days.—Lisbon and its Laureats, Vathek and Childe Harold.—Lord Carnarvon on Mafra and its marble halls.—Monasticism and Monarchy.—Aspect and Attributes of the Lusitanian Capital and its Vicinage.—Portuguese Millers and the Grinding process among the Grain Growers.—A 'bold peasantry, their country's pride,' the same everywhere.—Native memorabilia of the earthquake, and Anglo reminiscence thereof.—Anatomical offerings extraordinary.—The hic jacet of Tom Jones, and eke of Roderick Random.—Memento Mori, with admonitions to the Living.—Portuguese peculiarities.—Personal and political economy.—Fiscal fatuities.—Market-place notabilia.—Lisbon society.—Clubs and Cookery.—Tea and Turn-out.—Friars, Females, Fashions, and so forth, Operatic and Terpsichoratic.—Lusitanian fidalgos, or Portuguese Peers in Parliament.—Portugal the Paradise of Protectionists and Poverty.—Free-trade the only corrective of such calamities.—Court Circulars, Conventions, and Commanders.—Few books about Portugal, and necessity for more.—Hints from the newest, including the Oliveira Prize Essay.—A man's house something like a castle in Lisbon, at the cost of a cottage ornée.—Diplomatic and Consular Memoranda.

> On, on the vessel flies, the land is gone,
> And winds are rude in Biscay's sleepless bay.
> *Three days are sped, but with the fourth,* anon,
> New shores descried make every bosom gay,
> And Cintra's mountain greets them on their way,
> And Tagus, dashing onward to the deep,
> His fabled golden tribute bent to pay;
> And soon on board the Lusian pilots leap,
> And steer 'twixt fertile shores where yet few rustics reap
>
> CHILDE HAROLD.

INNUMERABLE as are the craft of every calibre and formation,— sail, steam, and screw,*—by which this favourite and familiar route is traversed. seldom had the voyager seen in its course a vessel of dimensions similar to those of the Argentina, paddle-wheel, in which I had embarked, constructed at Birkenhead by Mr. John Laird, to run between Monte Video and Buenos Ayres. She is, (or rather was, for alack, she is now a thing of the past,) 185 feet long by 21 feet beam, and with very fine, hollow lines; her engines of 120-horse power, by Fawcett, Preston, and Co. Intended for river work, and of a light draught of water, it was hardly to be expected that in ocean steaming, when compelled to carry coals, provisions, and all the bulky and ponderous requirements of a long voyage, the same results could be obtained as in the comparatively tranquil waters of inland navigation; but under all the disadvantages of being so laden, and having to make way against a strong head-wind and heavy sea, our average speed to Cape Finisterre was nearly 12 knots. Subsequently, we had a more favourable wind, and canvas assisted us a little, until we

---

* According to the official returns for the twelvemonth ending March last, the amount of British tonnage entered inwards from Portugal consisted of 7 steam and 735 sailing-vessels; the total amount of both class of vessels being 71,536 tons. The amount of British tonnage cleared outwards for Portugal consisted of 7 steam and 716 sailing-vessels, the total amount of tonnage being 76,662. Great Britain receives nearly a half of all the exports of Portugal, and Portugal only receives one-fiftieth of all the exports of Great Britain. —It appears from M'Gregor's 'Synthetical View of Legislation,' that in 1851, the total amount of the exportations of Great Britain and Ireland was about £75,000,000, of which only £1,048,356 was to Portugal! being less than the amount sent by Great Britain and Ireland to Chili and Peru! Whereas, in the United States the consumption of British goods has doubled since 1841, and now amounts to nearly one-fifth of all the British manufactures exported.

made the Berlings, (bold islets standing out some half-dozen miles from the land, with a light-house upon them,) getting to our moorings in the Tagus, before dark, on the evening of the fourth day after quitting the Mersey.

It is impossible to conceive an easier navigation than that to Lisbon; when once across the Bay of Biscay and round Cape Finisterre, you make direct for the Berlings, and other high rocks more to seaward, called the 'Estellas' and 'Farilhoes de Velha.' There is plenty of spare room for any vessel to pass inside the Berlings, thus saving some distance; and from Cape Corvoeiro the coast tends inwards to the mouth of the Tagus,* presenting a succession of scenery, so novel and attractive, as at once to satisfy the spectator that the poetry of Byron and the poetic prose of Beckford,† have failed to exaggerate its beauties. Conspicuous among the latter, though it is the handiwork of man availing himself of nature in her picturesquest mood, stands out

* It is so needless to tell any one entering the Tagus, much less any one who has entered, how topographically accurate is the description in 'Childe Harold,' that the stanzas are quoted merely to save the reader the trouble of referring to the volume itself, in case he do not quite remember the lines:—

> The horrid crags, by toppling convent crown'd,
> The cork-trees hoar that clothe the shaggy steep,
> The mountain-moss by scorching skies embrown'd,
> The sunken glen, whose sunless shrubs must weep,
> The tender azure of the unruffled deep,
> The orange tints that gild the greenest bough,
> The torrents that from cliff to valley leap,
> The vine on high, the willow branch below,
> Mix'd in one mighty scene, with varied beauty glow.
>
> Then slowly climb the many-winding way,
> And frequent turn to linger as you go,
> From loftier rocks new loveliness survey,
> And rest ye at 'Our Lady's house of woe,'
> Where frugal monks their little relics show,
> And sundry legends to the stranger tell:
> Here impious men have punish'd been, and lo!
> Deep in yon cave Honorius long did dwell,
> In hope to merit Heaven by making earth a hell.

† Next to Byron, the great modern English literary name associated with this part of Portugal, and not merely from his residence here, but from his delightful and extraordinary pourtrayal of the conventual life of the neighbourhood, in his almost posthumous work, the 'Monasteries of Alcobaça and Batalha,' is he whom the noble bard alludes to in the well-known lines:—

the height-crowning, marble-built Mafra, termed the Escurial of Portugal, from its immensity, magnificence, and the diversity of its contents, consisting of a palace, a convent, and most superb church, whose six organs were pronounced by Byron to be the most beautiful he ever beheld in point of decoration, and was told that their tones corresponded to their splendour. The town of Mafra itself is a small place, 18 miles N.W. of Lisbon, containing about 3,000 inhabitants, and owes what importance it possesses to the celebrated regal and ecclesiastical edifice, constructed in its vicinity by John V., in pursuance of a vow that he would select the poorest locality in the kingdom, and, finding twelve Franciscan friars living in one hut here, he gave the preference to Mafra —a partiality which its position, if not its preeminent poverty, abundantly justifies.*

A cluster of shoals, called the bar, forms a semicircle at the

> On sloping mounds, or in the vale beneath,
> Are domes where whilome kings did make repair,
> But now the wild flowers round them only breathe,
> Yet ruin'd splendour still is lingering there,
> And yonder towers the Prince's palace fair
> There thou, too, Vathek ! England's wealthiest son,
> Once form'd thy Paradise, as not aware
> When wanton Wealth her mightiest deeds hath done,
> Meek Peace voluptuous lures was ever wont to shun

Beckford, as is well known, soon after his return to England, built the fairy-like structure of Fonthill Abbey, gorgeous as his own Caliph Vathek, and, like it, as unsubstantial; for, on its being sold to Mr Farquharson for some £40,000, about one-seventh of what it cost, [the catalogues describing its contents were in prodigious demand at a guinea a piece] it fell to the ground. He died in 1844, aged 84, and was father to the late Duchess of Hamilton, and father-in-law to the present Duke of Hamilton and Duchess of Newcastle.

* At this convent was educated Don John VI., grandfather to the late 'Lusian's luckless Queen,' who died in 1816 in Brazil, from the melancholy derangement from which Dr Willis, who had attended George III. for a similar malady, was unable to recover her. The young prince was placed here with the idea of his wearing the cowl as abbot, prior to attaining the highest ecclesiastical honours; but the unexpected death of his elder brother made him heir to the throne, which he afterwards filled. Of the suitability of the structure for so august an inmate, the late Lord Carnarvon, who visited it in 1827, says:—I rode through a bleak but not unpleasant country to Mafra. The convent and palace united constitute an immense pile of building, which excites admiration rather from its vast extent than from any architectural

BELEM CASTLE, LISBON.

mouth of the Tagus, but is seldom an obstacle to vessels entering, for there is generally abundance of water on it to float even the largest vessels, the least depth in the north channel, at low water, being 4 fathoms, and in the south, 6. The only time that any difficulty is encountered, is when the freshes, after heavy rains up the country, add their strength to that of the ebbing tide, which then runs out at the rate of seven or eight miles an hour, and encounters a gale from seaward, for this causes the water to break right across, and vessels must await the turn of the tide to get in ; but in other respects the approach appears very easy, scarcely any captain who has been there before requiring the services of a pilot. After the intricacies and dangers of our own (the St. George's) Channel navigation, with the miles of sandbank that have to be threaded in approaching Liverpool, such an entrance as that to Lisbon calls but for small skill indeed in seamanship, and almost the veriest tyro in boxing the compass might enact the part of Palinurus.

Passing up the Tagus there are numerous forts, palaces, and other imposing buildings, or at least what appeared to be such in the dim twilight that prevailed during our advance towards the Lusitanian capital. The most commanding object (whereof presently) among these is Belem Castle, near which we were visited by the health officers, and allowed to proceed to our moorings off Lisbon, or rather to those of the Royal Mail Company, which had

merits, and forms a quadrangle, measuring 760 feet from east to west, and 670 feet from north to south The church is situate in the centre, and three hundred cells are placed behind the choir ; the palace might perhaps contain without inconvenience all the courts of Europe The thermometer had risen to more than 90°, and it was indeed no common luxury to exchange such intolerable heat for the refreshing temperature of the convent galleries, which are built of stone, and are high, wide, dark, and apparently interminable Within those massive walls the fluctuations of the external atmosphere are never felt; and rarely indeed do any external sounds pierce through those mighty barriers The monks showed us the refectory, a spacious apartment, and the library, well stored with books.—Portugal and Galicia, with a Review of the Social and Political State of the Basque Provinces By the Earl of CARNARVON Third Edition —London. John Murray, Albemarle Street. 1848 been kindly lent until such time as our own are laid down. The rule at the Custom-house, in respect to vessels, is for the masters to enter them and declare whether their cargoes are destined to be landed in Lisbon or not; if this be doubtful, which was not our case, they ask to be put in *franquia*, that is, for leave to remain eight days in port until the point is decided. On obtaining this they proceed a little way up the river for the appointed period. From Belem to that part of the river which is opposite to the centre of the city, a distance of about four miles, the Tagus is some one and a half wide, and displays on its northern bank, mingled with the dark foliage of the orange and other trees, successive clusters of dwellings and churches, including the palaces of the Ajúda and of Necessidades, in which latter the court is generally held, and from it mostly are dated the royal decrees.

With but few exceptions, these buildings are white, which gives the city, at first sight, a much cleaner appearance than is presented on a nearer view. On the south side, which is hilly, but few buildings, unless we include a small fishing village near the mouth of the river, are visible, until the small town of Almada, opposite to the city, is reached, containing 4,000 inhabitants, and in whose vicinity is the gold mine of Adissa, which has been worked now for some years. A peculiar characteristic of the neighbourhood of Lisbon are the little mills with sails, gyrating away on every eminence, sometimes half a dozen within a few yards of each other, and they whisk round so merrily, as to be quite a pleasant feature in the landscape. It might be the land, *par excellence*, of Jolly Millers; for the floury sons of the Tagus seem to belong to the same race as their jovial brothers of the Dee, whose philosophic indifference to the opinion of the world has been made alike musical and memorable by Mr. Braham. That the Portuguese should be sprightly, however, is extremely surprising, seeing that they are ground into dust, almost as literally as their own grain, or at least, the growers thereof; for one who knows them well, writing during a visit as late as last year, (1853), says:—

They are a people much resembling in heartiness and good will our own Irish brethren: they are also most apt to learn, and, like the much calumniated sons of Erin, can work, and will work when they are properly encouraged and remunerated. They toil under a burning sun, half-naked and bare-headed, or in the winter under drenching rains and piercing cold, with naught else to protect them from the weather than a straw thatch, or cloak; and without other aliment at times than a lump of Indian-maize bread, and a mess of humble pottage, or, at others, the same bread, and a raw onion, with water from the brook as their only drink. *Couve gallego* (cow cabbage,) from their own little garden, a spoonful of oil from their own olive-tree, a handful of salt gathered from the rocks on the sea-shore, with crumbled Indian-corn bread, baked in their own oven, (which, as is still the case in Canada, is built outside every tenement,) form a stir-about, on which the labourer contentedly makes his principal or even-tide meal, after the toils of the day are over. Occasionally, he may indulge in a morsel of *bacalhao* (salt cod-fish), or a rancid sardine: but where the family is numerous, from year's end to year's end, they know not the taste of animal food.

There are but few wharves alongside of which vessels can take in and discharge their cargoes, so they lie at anchor in the stream, and those operations are performed by means of lighters. There are, nevertheless, some handsome quays, with convenient landing-places, of which those at the fish-market and the Caes Sodré are the most frequented; at the former, the scene being highly animated, particularly in the season for sardinhas, or sardines, which constitute a considerable proportion of the food of the lower orders. The handsomest quay is that which forms one side of Blackhorse Square (Terreiro do Paço), so called from the statue of Joseph the First on horseback in the centre; the other sides consisting of public buildings, viz., the Public Library, the Offices of the Ministers of State, the Custom-house, and, at the eastern extremity, the Exchange, being chiefly of marble, as, indeed, nearly all the principal edifices are. It makes a splendid promenade, where crowds of well-dressed persons may be seen, on the sultry summer evenings, walking, or seated on the stone benches, enjoying the cool air from the river, until a late hour. From this square, five parallel and level streets, in which are the best shops, lead to the Roçio—a large, open space surrounded by buildings, and appropriated to reviews, processions, &c., and where, on its northern side, at one time existed the odious Prison

PRAÇA DO COMMERCIO, LISBON.

of the Inquisition, adjoining the Palace of the same name, now no longer occupied, though sometimes visited on festive occasions by royalty. Just beyond are the public gardens, well laid out, and stocked with flowers and shrubs, that bespeak the luxuriance and brilliancy of the Lusitanian arboretum.

All this portion of the city is more regularly built than the remainder, and is situated just over the very spot that felt the effects of the terrible earthquake, traces of which are now and then met with, in the shape of patches of old pavement, in digging for the foundations of houses, &c.; though there are no traces of the successful storming of the city by the French, under Junot, in 1807, nor of its equally successful resistance of a similar attempt a couple of years afterwards. In the vicinity of the Hospital of St José are the ruins of a church, in which, embedded in the earth, were to be seen, some years since, if not now, skeletons, in various attitudes, of persons who formed the congregation at the time the catastrophe took place, which was, as the reader will recollect, when the greater number of the citizens were assembled at mass in the churches on All-Saints' Day, November 1st, in the ever-memorable year 1755—a circumstance that will probably account for the enormous number of 30,000 lives being lost; for, although 6,000 private dwellings were destroyed, the fatality could hardly have been so great but for the multitudes being assembled in the mode mentioned. The celebration of the festival, too, was otherwise the occasion of prodigious mischief; for, owing to the immense number of tapers in the churches, the curtains, drapery, and other combustible materials, caught fire, and a devastating conflagration swept the doomed city from end to end, carrying off what the convulsion had not already prostrated in ruin. Indirectly, however, the commemoration of the festival was productive of some good—at least to our countrymen in Lisbon; for, in order to avoid exciting religious prejudice during a fête so solemn in the Papal calendar, they had nearly all retired to their country houses, and but ten who remained in the city were killed, a fact which renders, if possible, more magnanimous the grant by the British parliament of £100,000 to the relief of the suffering Portuguese, immediately the dismal tidings arrived; news of like events, but not on such a scale, continuing to be received for a long time after, from various portions of the New World. As in the case of our own dear delightful ante-diluvian Chester, the older quarters of Lisbon city generally interest a stranger most, from their very irregularity; the streets being narrow, steep, and destitute of *trottoirs,* and the houses very lofty, ranging in height from five to as many as eleven stories, in each of which dwells a separate family, all using one staircase in common. Notwithstanding the seeming peril from this cause, in the event of another earthquake, the danger of the walls falling is considerably lessened by their being built with a strong framework of timber, dovetailed together, before the addition of brick or stone.

Some of the churches are very handsome, although the absence of steeples will perhaps cause them to be hardly so regarded by the majority of Englishmen, and, moreover, many are in an unfinished state, for want of funds. The one that probably astonishes unsophisticated Saxons most, is the Patriarchal Church, from the circumstance of the pillars which support the roof being covered with wax models of heads, arms, legs, &c.—the *naïf* native offerings of individuals, desirous of testifying their gratitude to the Virgin, for her cures of complaints affecting those corporeal adjuncts. In the church of St. Roque is a small chapel, containing imitations, in mosaic, of several pictures of the Italian masters. These, with the splendid decorations, consisting of lapis lazuli columns, candelabra in the precious metals, &c., are credibly estimated to have cost upwards of one million sterling. This vast expense, of course, could only have been in Portugal's most palmy days, when the genius of Albuquerque threw open the portals of the East, and showered 'barbaric pearl and gold' upon his noble king, Emanuel, rightly indeed called the 'Fortunate,' and deserving so to be, as worthily inheriting the throne of Alphonso the Victorious (son of the heroic Henry of Burgundy) who routed five Saracen monarchs at Ourique, and freed his country from the Moors. The British cemetery* (*Os aciprestes*), surrounding a neat chapel, is well worth a visit, including, in its attractions, a monument to Fielding who there lies buried. Few of our countrymen, who have the opportunity, ever fail to make a pilgrimage to the spot where rests all that is mortal of him who drew Partridge and Blifil, Squire Western and Sophia,

* The mention of the English burial-ground, in Lisbon, induces us to correct an error into which the recent religious persecutions in Italy have betrayed some of our countrymen at home, as to the supposed existence of such practices in Portugal. Such a mistake is perfectly natural, but it is wholly unfounded; for, though the religion of the state is strictly Roman Catholic, of the most unmitigated character, still, like Brazil, though unlike Spain, there is toleration for all religions, and no impediment thrown in the way of their being observed. A Portuguese resident in London, writing to a leading journal on the point raised in consequence of the iniquitous treatment of the Madiai and others by the Duke of Tuscany, says :—'The liberality and toleration of the Portuguese government towards Protestants, either resident or travelling, in Portugal, has existed for ages past. That line of conduct has never been altered, and for the truth of this assertion I appeal to the British Legation at Lisbon, and to the very numerous and respectable British commercial body connected with that country. A British subject has as much civil and religious liberty in Portugal as he can possibly enjoy in his own country. Christianity and civilization were first carried to Asia, Africa, and America, by that nation which his Lordship so much depreciates, and the door of that vast empire which Great Britain possesses in India was opened by the inhabitants of that soil.' The imputation on the religious liberality of Portugal excites some indignation in that country, and a letter from Lisbon, in one of the papers, at the beginning of the year, says :—Not only since the establishment of the constitution, but even during the absolute regime, a large measure of toleration was always allowed to all other religions. The English and German Protestants have long had churches and cemeteries of their own, and, unlike their brethren in Spain, are allowed to bury their dead with as much 'pomp and publicity' as they please. The only restriction imposed upon people of other persuasions is, that they shall not, by word of mouth, or in writing, revile and insult the established religion of the country. This restriction, which was formerly operative, has now, however, become a dead letter, the real religion of the liberal party generally being materialism, against which nobody here seems disposed to declaim. At the beginning of the present year, (1854), a statement, signed by many of the principal British residents in Oporto, appeared in the London journals, setting forth that the most unreserved liberty for the performance of Protestant Service, with any degree of publicity, was allowed in that city, and had been for a great number of years.

Parson Adams and Tom Jones—his tomb being as eagerly sought as is that of his brother humourist, Smollett, at Leghorn. Strange that two of the most essentially English of all our writers should have died and been entombed so far from their native land whose literature their genius has so long enriched, and will for ever continue to do so.

Besides the public buildings already mentioned, there are several well-managed hospitals, an arsenal, academies for instruction in the naval, military, and other sciences; the Castle of St George, used as a prison more than as a place of defence: museums; a noble national library, of 30,000 volumes, formed from those of the convents suppressed in 1835, and, lastly, the aqueduct of Alcantara, with thirty-six arches, a splendid structure, north of the city, supplying the greater part of the inhabitants with water, and so solid, that it withstood the shock of earthquake, which laid nearly all else in ruins. The central arch is of sufficient dimensions to allow of a three-decker, under full sail, passing through, were there water to float her.

The population of Lisbon is between 250,000 and 300,000, having increased rapidly of late years, though sadly thinned during Don Miguel's usurpation, owing to the wholesale murders which were then committed, the numbers obliged to serve in the army, and killed, and also the emigration so many hundreds, nay thousands, were compelled to have recourse to, in order to escape from his cruelties, and those of his satellites. The remembrance of these atrocities, however, would seem insufficient to deprive him of some partizans in the country yet, if we may judge by the intrigues in his favour that have supervened on the death of the queen.

A first visit to Portugal cannot fail to revive—in the minds of Englishmen—'memories of the past,' full of 'sweet and bitter fancies,' as being alike the spot where England, by her diplomatic fatuity, earned an immortality of ridicule, and, by her valour, an eternity of praise, thanks to the Great Duke and his troops, so many of whom fell in defence of those liberties, which, if what

CINTRA, NEAR LISBON.

survives here be a fair specimen, were certainly hardly worth the cost of preservation ;* for, even at this distance of time, how many families can recal the bereavements they sustained in that glorious struggle. Moreover, Portugal possesses a deep interest from the great deeds of its early navigators, already slightly adverted to None who sympathize with the noble qualities the mention of these heroic names conjures up can fail to deplore that the spirit of Vasco de Gama, Cabral, Camoens,† and many others, has not descended to succeeding generations, rendering the land their genius and patriotism had adorned what it might yet be made under an enlightened government, viz, one of the most prosperous countries in Europe. That it is not so, even after the mismanagement it has endured, and is enduring now, nearly as

> * Lo ! Cintra's glorious Eden intervenes
> In variegated maze of mount and glen
> Ah, me ! what hand can pencil guide, or pen,
> To follow half on which the eye dilates,
> Though views more dazzling unto mortal ken
> Than those whereof such things the bard relates,
> Who to the awe-struck world unlock'd Elysium's gates ?

Sir Wm Napier's correction, in his History of the Peninsular War, of the blunder about the supposed site of the convention, is well known, but deserves to be repeated —

"The armistice, the negotiations, the convention itself, and the execution of its provisions, were all commenced, conducted, and concluded, at the distance of thirty miles from Cintra, with which place they had not the slightest connection, political, military, or local, yet Lord Byron has gravely asserted, in prose and verse, that the convention was signed at the Marquis of Marialva's house at Cintra, and the author of ' The Diary of an Invalid,' improving from a poet's discovery, detected the stains of the ink spilt by Junot upon the occasion "

> † As when to them who sail
> Beyond the Cape of Hope, and now are past
> Mozambic, off at sea, north-east winds blow
> Sabean odours from the spicy shore
> Of Araby the blest —Paradise Lost, Book iv

The voyage from Portugal to India was, in those days, more perilous than will easily be believed in these. The seas swarmed with pirates, shipwrecks were dreadfully frequent, and even when these dangers were escaped, the common mortality was so great, that Vieyra says—' If the dead, who had been thrown overboard between the coast of Guinea and the Cape of Good Hope, and between that cape and Mozambique, could have monuments placed for them each on the spot where he sunk, the whole way would appear like one continued cemetery ' Hyperbolical as this is, it shows how enormous the expenditure of life must have been, which could thus be spoken of in the pulpit! The ship in which Camoens sailed was the only one of the fleet which reached its destination bad as ever, is a matter of never-ending wonderment to those who know its means and appliances for advancement in the scale of nations. As regards myself, desire for personal authentication on the spot of what I had known from others, imparted an additional zest to my visit, from long acquaintance with the Brazils, even in the time of the grandfather of the late Queen, when the present splendid South American empire was a struggling colony of the now enfeebled and decaying parent kingdom. Hence I was prepared to look with a favourable eye on all that came under my notice in the capital of Portugal—a disposition enhanced by the first glance I had an opportunity of bestowing upon it; for, seen from the river on a bright sunny morning, Lisbon's strikingly picturesque aspect and position reminded me strongly both of Bahia and Rio Janeiro, a portion of the city being built, like them on low ground, hills, covered in every direction with handsome structures of variegated colours, chiefly white, rising like an amphitheatre behind; whilst the red-tiled roofs, green verandahs, and other fanciful decorations, lend to the whole a very foreign, almost tropical, but extremely pleasing appearance.

Unfortunately, the parallel between the capital of Portugal and the metropolis of her flourishing transatlantic offspring further holds good, as, on landing, much of the pleasing illusion vanishes:

> For whoso entereth within this town,
> That, sheening far, celestial seems to be,
> Disconsolate will wander up and down,
> 'Mid many things unsightly to strange ee,
> For hut and palace show like filthily,
> The dingy denizens are rear'd in dirt,
> Ne personage of high or mean degree
> Doth care for cleanness of surtout or shirt,
> Though shent with Egypt's plague, unkempt, unwash'd, unhurt.

Nor are you greatly disposed to make allowances for the cause of your topographical disenchantment, as you find yourself a mere object of fiscal surveillance—obliged to be set ashore at the Custom-house, like a biped bale of merchandise, and have your hat or umbrella scanned as if they ought to be subjected to duty, like everything else, animate and inanimate, that approaches these most absurdly protected waters. Very soon, however, mere chagrin at such petty personal annoyances deepens into gloom, as you observe the mournful absence of that incessant activity you expect to meet with in so large and important a place. The fatal spell of lethargy and exclusiveness seems to be laid upon everything and everybody:—the very carriages and public conveyances (at least a large portion) are redolent of the past century, and all idea of locomotion is put to flight at the sight of them; and just the same is the case with the owners. Torpidity pervades the whole population, from the infant in arms, who is too lazy to laugh, to the cripple on crutches, who is too sluggish to grumble. An exception to this rule, however, is the market-place, where fruit, vegetables, the sardines already spoken of, and other odd articles, are brought for sale. The motley groups, with their baskets or little stalls, sheltered by umbrellas of all sizes and colours, are like so many fancy-fair Chinese, whom Portuguese a good deal resemble in bodily configuration, as well as in other attributes equally little spiritualised, however Celestial. The kaleidoscopic tableau going on here is a relief to the monotony of other places of resort, and so vividly impresses the stranger that he fancies the performers in the scene must be foreigners, and not 'natives and to the manner born.' The theatrical air of the whole thing is not a little heightened, in his opinion, on finding that no sooner has the clock told one, than, like one o'clock, they all have to pack up their wares and depart till next day, in preparation for the business whereof the market is thoroughly cleaned and put in order. This regulation might be advantageously adopted in regions where the mention of the word Portuguese, especially in connection with cleanliness, immediately superinduces a spasmodic agitation in the hearer's nose, if indeed he can keep his countenance at all.

But Portuguese society, as I happen to know very well, from long and varied experience, is extremely agreeable in many places; and certainly the natives of the old country are exceedingly hospitable to strangers. There are several clubs, at the balls of one of which, the Foreign Assembly-rooms, all the rank and fashion of the capital are to be seen, to the number of several hundreds. I had the gratification of being introduced at the Lisbon Club. The house had been formerly, like so many similar institutions in London, a nobleman's palace. Although not on so grand a scale, it possesses superior accommodation to most places of the kind amongst us, and if the Portuguese keep no Soyer, Francatelli, or Ude, with a *batterie de cuisine* corresponding in magnitude and diversity to the celebrity of these professors of the finest art—that of giving a good dinner—they have a social party of an evening * when a piquant and substantial tea is provided for those who wish to sacrifice to the 'Chinese nymph of tears, Bohea.' The original taste of the Portuguese, who were the first to introduce the beverage to Europe, long before Mr. Pepys drank his 'cup of China drink,' [1661,] still survives, as well as the taste for coffee, the berry of Mocha being a favourite among the offspring of the victims of the Arabs. Chocolate, also, is a very popular beverage, and is consumed in considerable quantities at breakfast and supper, the two principal meals among the majority of Portuguese. The upper classes dress like those of other European capitals, but the lower order of females still retain the cloak and hood peculiar to this part of the Peninsula. There is not, however, so much difference now between the costume of the population and that of other cities, as the cowls, sandals, and rope belts of the friars, are no longer to be seen; for, as is well known, all the religious orders (not

* The middle classes promenade with their families until the sun begins to have effect, when they return to breakfast and to business. Dinner is usually served from noon till 2 p m , and consists of sopa, vaca cozida, e arroz, (soup, boiled beef, and rice,) with occasionally hum prato do meio (a dish of roast for the centre). Potatoes are seldom or never used, excepting in the kitchen. Fish is only eaten on fast-days, and the delicious sardine (because common and plentiful) shares the fate of the potatoes. The common vin ordinaire of the country is drunk at table out of small tumblers, being supplied from a neighbouring tenda (wine-store) daily or hourly, as it may be required, at a price never exceeding 2d per pint. Fine old bottled wine (such as we are acquainted with) is altogether unknown in Portugal, and it would be almost as rare to find in any house a couple of dozen bottles of wine, as it would be to discover as many books. Fire-places have not yet become general in dwelling-houses. In cold weather, gentlemen in society wear capotes (large cloth cloaks), and ladies wrap up in thick shawls. Dinner-parties are quite uncommon, but social evening meetings, where tea and simple biscuits are the only refreshments, are of constant occurrence.—*Forrester's Essay.*

those of nuns) were suppressed in 1835. There is a strong partiality for gaudy colours and trinkets; but that is passing away.

Though, generally speaking, the female population of Portugal are not of very prepossessing appearance, especially the humbler classes, whose naturally swarthy complexion is embrowned by exposure to the sun, there are few capitals in Europe where more perfect specimens of beauty are to be seen than in Lisbon; and what enhances the effect their somewhat unexpected presence produces is, that they are almost invariably *blondes*, therein differing from most of their Iberian sisterhood on the other side of the Douro, especially those of Cadiz, of whom the noble lord, already quoted, says that they are the Lancashire Witches of Spain. But the other noble lord, whom we have also quoted—and we certainly can corroborate all he says, from our individual experience in Brazil, of the classes he speaks of—observes: 'If I could divest myself of every national partiality, and supppose myself an inhabitant of the other hemisphere, and were asked in what country society had attained its most polished form, I should say in Portugal This perfection of manner is, perhaps, most appreciated by an Englishman : Portuguese politeness is delightful, because it is by no means purely artificial, but flows, in a great measure, from a national kindness of feeling. The restless feeling, so often perceptible in English society, hardly exists in Portugal; there is little prepared wit in Portuguese society, and no one talks for the mere purpose of producing an effect, but simply because his natural taste leads him to take an active part in conversation. Dandyism is unknown among their men, and coquetry, so common among Spanish women, is little in vogue among the fair Portuguese. They do not possess, to the same extent, the hasty passions and romantic feelings of their beautiful neighbours; but they are softer, more tractable, and equally affectionate. Even when they err, the aberrations of a married Portuguese never spring from fashion or caprice, seldom from vanity, and, however culpable, are always the result of real preference. Certainly, with some exceptions, the women are not highly educated; they feel little interest, on general subjects, and, consequently, have little general conversation. A stranger may, at first, draw an unfavourable inference as to their natural powers, because he has few subjects in common with them; but, when once received into their circles, and acquainted with their friends, he becomes delighted with their liveliness, wit, and ready perception of character.' I quote this passage, believing from all I heard and observed in Lisbon, that it is an accurate summary of the Portuguese character there; that it is nearly equally applicable, in a great degree, to Portuguese society in Madeira; and, knowing that it is so, in respect to Portuguese society in Brazil.

The places of amusement consist of five theatres, including the opera-house, where, as the London and Parisian *dilettanti* well know, many excellent singers make their *début*: the getting up the scenery, &c., are inferior to few establishments of the kind anywhere, and the prices are very moderate. It is called San Carlos, and it is scarcely inferior in any respect, either in its architectural extent or the liberality of its appointments, to its more famous Neapolitan namesake. Madame Castellan—herself, I believe, a fellow-countrywoman of Inez de Castro, whose portrait she greatly resembles—has been the principal lyric artiste during the past season. There is also a building for bull-fights, which, though perhaps as much a national sport as in Spain, is not pursued with the same passionate ardour, nor with the same skill, as is displayed by professors of the tauro-machiac art in the sister country.

I also attended a sitting of the two Chambers, which appeared to be conducted with great decorum, but, at the same time, without that listlessness or buzzy-fussiness which pervades our own Senate when a bore or a nobody happens to be on his legs. The accommodation for members is at least as good as ours. To be sure, it could not possibly be much worse, if we may judge from those most qualified to form an opinion—the members themselves; for, what with the perpetual complaints about pestilent smells, hot blasts, freezing draughts, blinding light, and sightless darkness, o ie would imagine that the British Senate-house was constructed to serve as a 'frightful example' of deleterious architecture. The wonder is, that any M P. has the face to approach a life-insurance office, at the beginning of a session, without being prepared with a 'doubly hazardous' premium on his 'policy,' knowing that he is going to talk, or listen to the talk, of politics for some six months; and, certainly, the looks of many of our law-makers can be consolatory to none but coffin-makers and residuary legatees. Not so with the Portuguese Conscript Fathers, nearly all of whom seemed as hale as new moidores out of the mint both as to stamina, complexion, and sensibility. The enormous building where they meet (the old convent of San Bento) contains all the needful official and red-tape-ical departments In the Upper Chamber, the Patriarch occupied the chair, in habiliments not unlike those of the Bishop of Oxford, when enrobed in his costume of Chancellor of the Order of the Garter; and it was curious to see an epitome of our own admixture of the ecclesiastical with the temporal system of legislation, in the House of Lords, carried out in this Portuguese conjunction of spiritual with lay law-makers.

In vain you look in the Tagus for that forest of shipping which should fringe the watery highway to, and ought to constitute the leading feature in, so fine a port—the capital of a country the once nautical genius of whose people is expressed in the only poem in any language that makes adventures on the deep its theme. A few stray vessels here and there, with river and fishing boats, and those singular latine sails, that so strike the stranger,* some steamers and Government vessels, were all that could now be seen on the bosom of the river, so famed amongst the

* These peculiar latine sails are exquisitely beautiful when seen in profile and, when beheld in front, resemble a butterfly perched on a dark ground with expanded wings —*Carnarvon*   British naval architects will probably be surprised to hear that the Portuguese craft of every kind are all prime built and beautiful models, the elegance of their lines being a source of admiration to every critic The Oporto fishing-boats, in particular, are fine specimens of the country's capacity for this sort of excellence, and, when under sail, fly through the water at the rate of 12 to 14 knots an hour.

ancients for its golden attributes, not because of its auriferous sands,* but because of the affluent tide of its teeming commerce—that port whence, in after ages, though now ages long ago, went forth those expeditions which brought much of Asia into comparative contiguity with Europe, and discovered, and long held so much of, the finest portion of the New World. For a wonder, not a 'speck of power' of that nation, whose commerce rose as Lusitania's fell, not an English man-of-war, ubiquitous in every water, and very often present, and too long at a time, in most unnecessary numbers, in these waters in particular, was to be seen, though Admiral Corry's squadron, containing many of the finest and latest built men-of-war in our navy, including the 'Duke of Wellington,' and now with Napier in the Baltic, has since been there. Their absence, however gratifying to financial economists and advocates of non-intervention in politics, helped to complete the triste and dreary air of the empty mart and shipless bay. The cause of this poverty of trade must be obvious to all, even to enlightened Portuguese. The Government, blind to all experience elsewhere, deaf to the supplications of common sense and even self-interest, draw a kind of cordon round the little trade they still possess, and encumber it with such a net-work of preposterous restrictions, as actually to squeeze the life-blood out of it, or, rather, altogether arrest its circulation, which is the same thing in the end, as regards the vitality of commerce. The evil extends to every ramification of industrial pursuit; and one half of the population live upon a system that seems to have been invented to exclude, instead of encouraging business to come to their shores.

* In the days of Pliny, we are told, the provinces of Minho, Galicia, and Asturias paid not less than a million and a half octaves of gold to the Roman Empire, as a tribute on the ore extracted from various mines then in active operation, and yet, in the present day, the revenues derived by the Portuguese Government from all their mines does not amount to more than £72 17s. The Romans worked mines of gold, silver, iron, lead, coal, antimony, copper, quicksilver, bismuth, arsenic, and tin, in Portugal: and Faria e Souza graphically remarks, 'Hardly is there a river, or mountain-base that it laves, which does not cover precious stones and grains of gold.' This language may be considered poetic, but there is no doubt that 'le sol de Portugal est essentiellement metallifere,'—that metals abound throughout the whole country, but the mines are not worked; neither can their value be correctly ascertained, in the absence of every means of transport, and internal communication.—*Forrester.*

Hence, it need hardly be said, that smuggling is the most profitable trade going; and a large and rapidly increasing business in that line is carried on, along the frontier in particular

If Colonel Sibthorpe, Mr. Newdegate, and the remainder of that Spartan band of fifty-nine, who followed the phantom of Protection into the lobby of the House of Commons a couple of years ago, finding that the sun of England has indeed for ever set, as they so often anticipated, desire to bask in the beams of unmitigated monopoly, by all means let them hie hither forthwith; and they will behold one realm, at least, that carries out their views to the utmost possible extent. By way of apparently bolstering up native industry, Portugal fosters a few stray manufacturing establishments, and farms out monopolies of certain articles (tobacco and soap for instance) to parties who, in the rigorous exercise of their privileges, put another and most effectual drag-chain on the march of commerce. The fruits of such policy are but too apparent; for even the neighbouring state of Spain, so long the synonyme of every fiscal fatuity, but now awaking to a true sense of what it owes to her glorious maritime associations, and to her present and perspective well-being, is taking away a large portion of Portuguese traffic, by judiciously reducing her tariff, promoting railway enterprise, and gradually adopting those liberal views, without whose practical recognition now every country must lapse into almost primeval barbarism Undoubtedly an extenuation of the imbecility of Portugal is her complete dependence and reliance on her colonies so long, for while she enjoyed a monopoly of them she flourished at their expense. Now things are reversed, and Portugal cannot bring herself to adopt the only remedy, free-trade and unrestricted commerce, in its largest and fullest extent These would soon fill her ports with shipping, raise rents, augment revenue, and place her in a position worthy of the countrymen of Cabral, and of the *prestige* which he and so many of his cotemporaries and followers so long secured her. That she has an aptitude for commerce is well known; for, though it was long deemed degrading, and even criminal, in high caste Portuguese, to meddle in commercial matters, or to intermarry or associate with those who did, there is scarcely any 'Change in the world at the present day that does not number a Lisbon or Oporto merchant among its ablest members.

A stay of two days is a short time to enable a stranger to appreciate fully the merits of a large place like Lisbon; but the defects in her national fiscal system as here manifested, at the very fountain head of the intelligence and influence of the empire, and its mischievous tendency in retarding prosperity, are unmistakeable. The handwriting on the wall requires no interpreter, it points out approaching decay, unless Portugal alters her system before it is too late, and determines to go with the stream of events and the destinies of the world. The real hope for the country still points in the direction of Brazil; not only because of the peculiar weight of example in that quarter, where prosperity has progressively and unvaryingly followed every step in the path of commercial and political enlightenment—every assimilation to the existing English system of mercantile polity—but from the circumstance of the affluence of Brazil healthily reacting upon, and wakening up the energies of the old country to join *pari passu* in the march with her vigorous progeny. In a trading, especially in a passenger-trading sense, the connection between the two is still important, and is every day becoming more so, through Anglo-Brazilian enterprise, (of which the Liverpool Company I have the honour to belong to affords the most prominent instance yet), and is likely to be vastly improved by the establishment of direct steam navigation, chiefly carried on by native and South American capital. The principal promoter of this is Mr. Moser, well known for enterprise of a like kind in the navigation of the Minho, from which river to the Guadiana a screw steamer now plies.

Most of the *bourgeoisie* of Brazil were either born in Portugal or are descendants of Portuguese. Shop-keeping is a business these Peninsulars fully understand, especially those from Oporto; particularly in everything pertaining to trinkets, articles of jewellery, and goldsmith's-work, the Portuguese being therein cunning workmen, though for the most part, regarded as indifferent carpenters, shoemakers, and the like, at least by British employers After realizing money abroad, they naturally find their way to Portugal; where, if even for a season, they enjoy themselves as only children of the South or of the tropics can when they have the means; or spend the remainder of their days where their fathers lived and died before them. They will soon have the invaluable advantage of the steamers of no less than three companies calling at Lisbon, including the 'Luso-Brazileira,' which is also composed of Portuguese and Brazilian shareholders. These, let us hope, will prove the immediate harbingers of that good time which can alone be brought about by the multiplication of such instruments of a national good; for it must be obvious to every one who knows Portugal, or the Portuguese abroad, that what is wanted is abundance of communication by steam, both by sea and land, railways, and free-trade, or some approximation to it. With these she may resume her position amongst the nations, and share with her oldest ally, England, the benefits arising from a mutually advantageous intercourse.

Respecting the Royal Family, during my stay at Lisbon, when there was, of course, every apparent prospect of a long, if not a very tranquil and happy reign for the late Queen, I learnt that they kept themselves as retired and quiet as their exalted station would permit, appearing little in public, but understood to be busy in those plots and intrigues, suspicion of which on the part both of the people and the upper classes, deprived her Majesty of much of that popularity which her many excellent qualities were calculated personally to secure her. What may be the course that her husband, the Regent, will pursue, or that may be pursued by her son when he attains his legal majority in 1858, it is of course impossible to foresee. His young Majesty is now in the course of making a tour through Europe, chiefly with a view, it is said, of finding a partner for his throne; and rumour points to one of the house of Coburg to which his father belongs, viz., a daughter of the King of the Belgians. This alliance, though otherwise eligible in itself, is deemed by some politicians likely to aggravate the troubles of the country, by making it a hot-bed of extraneous intrigue, in addition to the domestic Miguelite plottings that appear chronic in Portgual.

There are, as already mentioned, several royal palaces, but few of them completely finished, or ever likely to be so, owing to the limited state of the civil list and the reluctance of the Cortes to grant supplies for such purposes. The Palace of Ajuda is a truly regal building, whose external magnificence at least, fills every one with regret that it should so far resemble so many others, of vast pretensions and undoubted beauty, as to remain incompleted, and in consequence, unoccupied. Visitors to the Court are generally located in a pretty marine palace, with a terrace and garden facing the river, at Belem, the town of which name contains about 5,000 inhabitants. In its vicinage is the burial-place of many of the earlier Portuguese monarchs; it possesses also, in addition to the castle and custom-house already mentioned, and a singular-looking fortress, some other public institutions of note, including a high-school, a convent, and the largest iron-foundry in Portugal, together with a noble church, built to commemorate the memorable departure of Vasco de Gama on his great voyage, as so beautifully alluded to by the national poet.

It may not be superfluous to caution the young or casual reader not to confound this town with one somewhat similarly pronounced, Baylen, in Spain—a spot that sounds in French ears pretty much as Cintra does in ours. And for much the same reason—the blundering incapacity of those charged with the conduct of the transactions that took place, almost simultaneously, in the same year, and within a month of each other; except that the former, having had priority of occurrence, rendered the latter more inexcusable. It was in July, 1808, that 14,000 French, commanded by Dupont and Wedel, being defeated by 25,000 Spaniards under Pena and Compigny, Dupont's entire division of 8,000 men laid down their arms—the beginning of the French disasters in Spain, as lending courage to the whole native population to pursue that system of resistance which in the end, aided and directed by British valour and science, rendered nugatory all the efforts of the invader permanently to subdue the country. Of Belem, the recent military celebrity is not great, the two chief incidents in its history being its capture by the French, the year before the occurrence just named; and, secondly, its capture under the troops of Don Pedro, in 1833. What lends its real historic, or at least archæologic interest to the place, is its propinquity to the remains of some of the finest Moorish architecture in the world, the Alhambra itself scarcely excepted; and these alone ought to suffice to render a trip fashionable among our *ennuyéd* tourists, to whom almost all the remainder of Europe is nearly as well known as the beach at Brighton or the Westmoreland lakes. Notwithstanding the charm to British ears of the words Busaco, Vimiera, Badajos, Braga, Torres Vedras, and the Douro, Portugal is a *terra incognita* to the pic-nicish and Pickwickian tribe, and altogether exempt from the remonstrance of the *blasé* bard—

> And is there then no earthly place,
> Where we can rest, in dream Elysian,
> Without some curst, round English face,
> Popping up near, to break the vision?
> 'Mid northern lakes, mid southern vines,
> Unholy cits we're doom'd to meet;
> Nor highest Alps nor Apennines
> Are sacred from Threadneedle Street!
> If up the Simplon's path we wind,
> Fancying we leave this world behind,
> Such pleasant sounds salute one's ear
> As—'Baddish news from 'Change, my dear!'

But how can it be wondered that Portugal should be a yet untrodden Eden to the tourist, seeing that it is the only country, or tract of country, in Europe, or on the confines thereof, from Odessa to Iceland, that Murray hasn't hand-booked? The 'Anak of Booksellers,' who has 'done' the Pyramids and the Pyrenees, Styria and Finland, Whitechapel and Wallachia, the Dnieper and the Nile, has left Portugal undone; for it cannot be called doing it, in the Albemarle-street sense of the term, to devote to it a few small pages of large type, and call them 'Hints.' Nevertheless, far below the Murrayan standard as that is, still it will be useful, as being likely to incite travellers thitherward ;* and then the great publisher will, doubtless, provide for their use some Head capable of turning out a sizeable and seasonable octavo of reading as delightful as Borrow and as instructive as Ford has done for the scarcely more romantic region the other side of the Guadiana. Meanwhile, calling attention to that one‡ of the 'Hints' which tells how others may be taken, as to the London means of getting there, in addition to those still better Liverpool means furnished by our South American Steam Company, it is well to apprise the reader, desirous of the latest and best information about Portugal, that it will be found in the extremely agreeable and attractive volume† which owes its origin to the munificence and patriotism

---

* Hints to Travellers in Portugal, in Search of the Beautiful and the Grand. With an Itinerary of some of the most Interesting Parts of that Remarkable Country.—London. John Murray, Albemarle Street. 1852.

† The Olivena Prize-Essay on Portugal with the Evidence Regarding that Country taken before a Committee of the House of Commons in May, 1852; and the Author's Surveys of the Wine-Districts of the Alto-Douro, as Adopted and Published by order of the House of Commons. Together with a Statistical Comparison of the Resources and Commerce of Great-Britain and Portugal. By Josh James Forrester, Wine-Grower in the Alto-Douro.—London. John Weale, 59, High Holborn. John Menzies, Edinburgh. Coutinho, Oporto. 1852.

‡ There is scarcely any difficulty now in going to Portugal, for a steamer sails from Southampton for Lisbon on the 7th, 17th, and 27th of every month, or on the following day, when any of those days should fall on a Sunday, and generally enters Vigo Bay in three days, and, weather permitting, calls off Oporto, and arrives in five or six days at Lisbon, from which city a steamer occasionally sails for Oporto, at which place the traveller is recommended to commence his excursions, the province of Minho excelling all others in Portugal in whatever is fertile and picturesque, and being, equal, if not superior, in grandeur to the district of the Estrella Mountains. The ordinary mode of travelling is on horses or mules, which can be hired for about 5s. 6d. per day, including their food, but the arrieros who accompany them must be maintained at the cost of him who hires them, and he likewise expects to receive a gratuity. The money of the country is calculated in reis, and taking the mil rei, or 1,000 reis, to be equal to 4s. 6d., the value of the current coin will be nearly as follows:—*In Silver*. The Cruzado *novo*, or 480 reis = 2s. 2d., the 12 Vintem piece, or 240 reis = 1s. 1d., the 6 Vintem piece, or 120 reis = 6½, the 3 Vintem piece, or 60 reis = 3¼d., the testoon, or 100 reis = 5¼d., the Half Testoon, or 50 reis = 2¼d.—*In Gold*. Moidore, or 4,800 reis = £1 1s. 8d., the small gold piece, or 5000 reis = £1 2s. 6d., the gold piece, or 8000 reis = £1 16s. The English sovereign circulates in Portugal for 4500 reis. The copper coins in general circulation are the following:—The 5 reis, equal to little more than 0¼d.; the 10 reis, equal to little more than 0½d., the 20 reis, or Vintem, equal to little more than 1d., the 40 reis, or Pataca, equal to little more than 2d.

of the accomplished member for Pontefract, Mr. Oliveira, who, sprung of the ancient Lusitanian stock himself, and numbering among his ancestors the Pombals, de Castros, Tojals, and Thomars, has laboured assiduously, and most successfully, in disseminating among the most intelligent and influential minds of either country a correct knowledge of what conduces to the commercial prosperity of both. Towards this end nothing can be more effectual than a careful study of the admirable essay alluded to below, and from which some few of the foregoing facts are taken. Indeed, we would fain hope that, at least some of the excellent arguments it addresses to the Portuguese government have already produced a good effect; for, in the speech to the Cortes by the Regent, in January last, there is great promise not only of railway encouragement, but regulations we have spoken of being relinquished, such as the monopoly on salt, and even that on tobacco is likely soon to be abandoned. Improvements of a similar kind are to be extended to Madeira.

Our political relationship with Portugal, from the personal family alliances between the two countries, and from other causes, has of late years been kept up at great expense ; and, according to some critics, with very little good to any but the individuals at whose instance and on whose behalf British interference has taken place, the Portuguese population being understood to be as little pleased with its effects as English taxpayers are enamoured of its expense. Ostensibly our diplomatic and consular corps now in Portugal consists of the following members, and at the salaries annexed to their names —Envoy extraordinary and minister plenipotentiary, Rt Hon Sir Richard Pakenham, K.C B , salary £4000 per ann ; and house-rent £500, secretary of legation. W R. Ward, salary £500; paid attache, Jos Hume Burnley, £250, unpaid attachés, Hon. W. G Cornwallis Elliot, and Hon Francis Pakenham Consuls —Lisbon, William Smith, £600; vice-consul, Jeremiah Meagher, £300; Oporto, Edwin Johnston, £500; Loanda, Geo Brand, vice-consul, £50; St Michael (Azores) T. C. Hunt, consul, £400 ; Fayal, J Minchin, vice-consul, £100; Terciera, J. Read, vice-consul, £100. Of the officers at Madeira and Cape Verds, (Portuguese possessions) due mention will be made under those heads. The Portuguese diplomatic and consular staff in England consists of :—Envoy extraordinary and minister plenipotentiary, Count de Lavradrio, 12, Gloucester Place, Portman Square; secretary of legation, Chevalier Pinto de Soveral; attachés, E. F. de la Figaniere, J. C. Stone, and Geo Manders ; consul-general, F. J. Vanzeller, 5, Jeffrey Square, St Mary Axe; consuls Liverpool, Almeida Campos; Bristol, Anf. B. de Mascarenhas; Cork, Geo Manders

In concluding this brief chapter, which is, unfortunately, necessarily much more brief than the subject warrants, we have only to add, that should its perusal, or that of the several works already enumerated, induce readers to visit Lisbon in search of pleasure, and more especially those in search of health, the important item of house-rent will be found almost fabulously moderate compared with any other capital in Europe, and, I should imagine, in the world. A perfect palace, in the literal meaning of the term, may be had for £100 a year, containing suites of rooms in which a coach and four might be turned. Provisions and all the produce of the country are exceedingly cheap, but all imported articles are equally dear, because of the absurd protective system already spoken of, which permits and encourages native manufacturers to make the worst articles at the highest price, thus of course entailing the most limited consumption, and restricts purchases of all commodities that can possibly be dispensed with. Amongst hotels, the Braganza, built on an eminence overlooking the Tagus, stands preëminent, and is part of the Braganza family estate. The bill of fare is attractive, and charges moderate, regret being felt that travellers by sea cannot go at once to such comfortable quarters, instead of to the vile Lazarette, to which they are now consigned *en route* from England or Brazil!

AJUDA PALACE, RESIDENCE OF THE ROYAL FAMILY OF PORTUGAL, NEAR LISBON.

THE LAUREL TREE, MADEIRA.

CHAPTER II.

LISBON TO MADEIRA.

Two more days' pleasant Paddling on the Ocean.—Approach to Madeira.—Charming aspect of the Island.—Unique boats and benevolent boatmen.—Pastoral progression in bucolic barouches extraordinary.—Personal appearance of the inhabitants.—Atmospheric attractions of Madeira, and absence of all natural annoyances.—The Vine-Blight and its consequences, present and prospective, on the people at home and the consumption of their wine abroad.—Funchal, and its urban and suburban et ceteras.—Romance and reality of the History of the Island, 'Once Upon a Time.'—Importance of English residents to the place.—Cost of living, and what you get for your money.—Royal and illustrious visitors.—Mercantile matters, and consular cordiality.—Grave Reflections in the British Burial Ground.

NOTE TO THE ILLUSTRATION.—Views of Funchal, of the English Burial-place, and other objects in Madeira, are so familiar, that in preference to any of them, there is here given, as being much less hacknied, one representing a small fort or outwork, called Loureiro, or the Laurel Tree, on the coast to the east of Funchal, being the first of the series copied from the portfolio of the gentleman to whom our volume is so much indebted for such privilege.

F

> Oh! had we some bright little isle of our own,
> In a blue summer ocean, far off and alone,
> Where a leaf never dies in the still blooming bowers,
> And the bee banquets on through a whole year of flowers,
> Where simply to feel that we breathe, that we live,
> Is worth the best joy that life elsewhere can give.
> The glow of the sunshine, the balm of the air,
> Would steal to our hearts, and make all summer there
> Our life should resemble a long day of light,
> And our death come on, holy and calm as the night.—MOORE.

OCEAN sailing, perhaps, does not present anything more delightful than the trip from Lisbon to this island in fine or moderate weather. We soon bade adieu to the Tagus, with its merry-going windmills, and its palaces and churches, the bold dome of the Coraçao de Jesus being the last visible in the horizon as we steamed away; and, on the second morning at daylight, made the Island of Porto Santo, which looks bleak and dreary enough, but has the repute of having some verdant spots upon it; and a small harbour called by the same name. Madeira, some 35 miles distant, was in sight a-head, its mountains peeping out of the clouds, and a couple of hours brought us up to the south side, along which we steamed. The hills were covered with innumerable cottages, and huts built amongst the vine plantations, which rise in ridges, nearly from the water's edge to the height of 2,000 feet; the best vine growths, no doubt, being found at about half that elevation. It is needless to say that the *coup d'œil* so presented is as charming as it is singular. Immediately after passing Brazen Head, the Bay of Funchal opened before us, and a more beautiful sight cannot well be conceived, the hills towering to a considerable altitude, dotted a long way up with pretty-looking villas and well cultivated gardens, until, reaching the town, these become merged in its compact mass. Funchal, which contains a population of some 20,000 inhabitants, bears the usual Portuguese characteristics of white or fancifully-coloured houses, many being lofty, with look-outs to the sea, forts, churches, &c. The Loo Rock, commanding the entrance of the bay, is very remarkable, being quite separated from the main land, which it there protects from the roll of the sea. Here we found lying in the roads, amongst other vessels, two American men-of-war, just come over from the African station to refresh, as well as the Severn steamer, coaling on her way from the Brazils to Lisbon and England. This opportunity enabled us to send home dispatches forthwith. An assemblage of those peculiarly strong-built boats, with double keels to protect them from being stove in by the tremendous swell that sets in-shore so frequently, soon came to us with offers of service, chiefly in the shape of miscellaneous matters for sale; and we found ourselves amongst a pushing, energetic race, anxious to trade and make money, with an earnestness that was quite refreshing. Many spoke tolerably good English, and showed evident signs of being accustomed to deal with our countrymen. Landing on the beach is sometimes a formidable operation here; but the boats, as we have said, are well adapted for all emergencies incident to the operation, whether performed by those in robust health, or, as is too frequently the case, by invalids, in almost the last stage preceding dissolution. The boatmen are very active and obliging on such occasions, and considerate to a degree that would be perfectly incredible to a Thames wherry-man at Gravesend. We were immediately beset by a crowd of applicants for favours in one shape or another, amongst whom were not a few beggars, although I believe they are prohibited from soliciting alms, and a very good institution exists for the helpless and houseless. Some of our passengers, with the precipitancy of English in all such matters the moment a foreign shore is reached, proceeded to test the vehicular conveniences of the island, by a drive in one of those extraordinary bovine sledges drawn by two bullocks, and which travel up the hills at a pace sufficiently surprising, considering the apparently sluggish conformation of the steeds.

I took a ramble over the town, and made sundry diplomatic calls; afterwards proceeding [aloft, as may be literally said,] to enjoy the hospitality of Mr. Blandy, who occupies a charming country seat about a mile up the hill, where there is a splendid view of the town and bay, as well as of the towering mountains above. One of the sleighs or sledges, just mentioned, carried us along a succession of steep hills very quickly, a mode of conveyance which, notwithstanding its primeval fashion, appears to be of recent date here. This *char rustique* of the mountains resembles, as nearly as possible, one of our turn-abouts at a fair, with two seats opposite to each other; but the most curious uses to which this odd contrivance is put, is in coursing down-hill by express train, as they call it. Two persons seat themselves side-by-side in the sledge, and an equal number of boys, holding a strap attached to it, commence running down the steep declivities at a pace that must be felt to be understood; but an idea of it may be formed by those who remember the Vauxhall illustration of centrifugal force, some years ago, when an unhappy monkey was placed in a carriage and shot down an inclined plain, at the bottom whereof was a huge wheel, over and around which the traveller and his vehicle were propelled, and brought to a stand-still after attaining a level on the other side. The Madeira roads are paved with sharp stones set very close together; so the machine glides downwards without meeting with any resistance, and, in ten minutes, descends a distance that takes half an hour or more to mount on horseback. It was the most curious sensation I ever felt; and, though assured of its safety, one cannot make the experiment for the first time without thoughts of an upset running in one's head, contact between which and the stones would not have been very agreeable. Mountainous countries are doubtless favourable to the promotion of personal activity; and certainly the way in which the natives go up and down the steep paths here, with burthens on their backs, especially in such a climate, is something remarkable.

It is no wonder that the English are fond of Madeira, but a very great wonder that far larger numbers do not resort thither, to pass the winter months, with the numerous facilities of steam navigation now presented to them. The climate, the total change of people and scenery, the teeming vegetation, yielding the produce both of Europe and the tropics, the picturesque disposal of the houses on the very ridges of the hills, with every regard to comfort and even luxury, all combine to render this a kind of earthly paradise, to which the seeming rhapsody at the head of our chapter is really only literally applicable. Here indeed nature showers down her choicest bounties: no fogs, miasmas, or even hurtful dews; atmosphere almost always translucent and bright; the thermometer in winter scarcely ever falling below 60 degrees; and where, during the hot summer months, a cool and comfortable retreat, of almost any temperature, may be found up the mountains. Lastly, there are no poisonous reptiles, merely a brown lizard, harmless to everything save the vines; frogs are quite a recent importation; and so far as I could learn, there are none of that numerous tribe of annoying insects which infest the tropical regions, only the familiar household flea, that makes himself at home everywhere.

Unfortunately, the dependence of the population and the staple of Madeira has been its vines, whose produce this year, as well as last, has totally failed, from some cause almost as inscrutable, or at least as incurable, and in its consequences nearly as calamitous, on a small scale, as the potato rot in isles nearer home. I could not have believed without seeing it —in every direction the grapes were withered up like parched peas, and, in many cases, the trees themselves dying. Such an extraordinary visitation has, I believe, never been known here before. It partakes very much of the same virulent character as the diseases that at times affect the cereal world, and something of the kind was experienced with terrible severity in the Canaries in 1704. Two years' failure of a vintage, in an island like Madeira, would be almost annihilation, if it were not for its other boundless vegetable resources; and, as in the case of the destruction of the Irish root, it is augured that much good may arise to the people from the increased stimulus to industry so occasioned, and their being induced not to place too great a dependence on any one product. Still, it is a melancholy sight to behold the support of a whole people struck down by such an inconceivable blight. Every means have been tried to arrest its progress, but without success; and, should it continue its ravages, Madeira wine bids fare to become greatly increased in value a few years hence, when, as a matter of course. it will be more in vogue and sought after, than has been the case for a long time back *

The streets of Funchal are narrow, but clean, and intersected by streams of water, brought also into nearly every large dwelling. Their silence, owing to the absence of vehicles, strikes the European stranger as extraordinary; especially at night, when he seems to be placed in a city of marionettes, as it were; and, from the presence of the palanquin, bearing fair occupants about, quite an oriental tinge is imparted to the aspect of the whole urban scene. Speaking of that, a note on the physical attributes of the Maderians; and we cannot do better than quote the authority of a gentleman*—perhaps we should say a lady, as it is doubtless her impressions in letter-press that are reflected on this point†—who is the latest authority on what may be called the *agremens* of the island.

There are aqueducts made to bring the water from the mountain side, and several deep gullies or ravines run through the town and empty themselves into the sea. These cavities being crossed by bridges, the sides have been built up at a considerable expense, and are covered with verdure, tropical and European, producing a most picturesque effect. They are also most beneficial in a sanitary sense, being in fact main arteries for circulating pure fresh air, as well as for carrying off the impurities.

Excepting epidemics, Madeira, both town and country, must naturally be the healthiest place in the world, for the reasons

---

* A Sketch of Madeira; containing Information for the Traveller, or Invalid Visitor. By EDWARD VERNON HARCOURT, Esq. With Sketches by Lady Susan Vernon Harcourt —London; John Murray, Albemarle Street. 1851

† You must not look for many pretty faces in Madeira after the age of thirteen: amongst the upper classes inertness, and amongst the lower, hard work, reduce the standard of beauty The upper class of women are hardly ever seen in the streets, save on their road to mass, or when going to pay a visit, on these occasions all the jewels, plate, and ribbons, of apparently very ancient families, are to be seen in full display. The ladies generally live on their balconies, watching passers-by. The English ladies, going to church draw forth many fair beholders and critics, and on Sundays the balconies are lined with native fashion. The glory of the Madeira women is their hair, which is of the richest growth and blackest hue, and their eyes, which are dark and bright —*Harcourt.*

already stated. The population of the island is estimated at upwards of 100,000, or, at least was so till lately; but there is a good deal of emigration going on, and owing to the late distress it is likely to increase materially, both to Demerara and the Brazils, where the natives prove to be most valuable labourers.

The history of Madeira, or at least its political history, is of no great importance. Like Brazil, it is named after its wood, and so is its capital, Funchal, from a species of fern abounding in still greater profusion than the magnificent timber. A romantic interest belongs to its early annals, as it was discovered, it is said, by Mr. Macham, an English gentleman, or mariner, who fled from England for an illicit amour. He was driven here by a storm, and his mistress, a French lady, dying, he made a canoe, and carried the news of his discovery to Pedro, King of Arragon, which occasioned the report that the island was discovered by a Portuguese, A D. 1345. But it is maintained that the Portuguese did not visit the place until 1419, nor did they colonise it until 1431.* It was taken possession of by the British in July, 1801; and again, by Admiral Hood and General (afterwards Viscount) Beresford, Dec. 24, 1807, and retained in trust for the royal family of Portugal, which had just then emigrated to the Brazils. It was subsequently restored to the Portuguese crown.

The residence of Englishmen here, is of course highly advantageous to the place, and they are welcomed, as they deserve to be, by a poor but industrious, and by no means abject or cringing, people. On the contrary, the population of all classes are remarkable for their frank and ingenuous bearing. Living† is reasonable;

---

* One of these traditions is very gracefully and attractively told by Mr. Charles Knight, in his agreeable volumes, published by Murray, a couple of months back, and entitled 'Once upon a Time.'

† Lodgings in Madeira are plentiful and good. For a family, the most comfortable plan is to take a *Quinta*, that is to say, a house with a garden, standing in the suburbs of the town The price asked for the season of six months varies according to their size, from £50 to £200 In such cases the tenant is supplied with everything but plate and house linen. For single persons the boarding-houses are least troublesome, as well as most economical. A bed-room, sitting-room, attendance, and board are obtained there for fifty dollars, or £10 8s. 4d a month. These houses are conducted on a liberal scale, and every English comfort is provided. If a *Quinta* is taken, a supply of servants, board, plate

and it is to be hoped that thousands, instead of hundreds, of our countrymen, will ere long find their way here. The visits of our late estimable Queen Adelaide, of the Dowager Empress of Brazils, and others of eminent station and corresponding means, are dwelt upon with gratitude, as they not only caused a considerable circulation of money, but did much good personally. In no part of the world can the bounties of nature, or the precious gift of health be so richly enjoyed, or in a manner so agreeable to Europeans, as here. The island has some little commerce with different places, but administered in a manner that renders all we said about Lisbon restrictions, monopolies, and mercantile impediments, applicable in an agravated degree, if that be possible; and, of course, until things mend there, no improvement can be looked for here. The trading portion of the community seem to be very social and friendly amongst themselves, although not mixing a great deal with the English, or rather, the English maintain their constitutional isolation from the natives, but with a rigidity which time is rapidly mitigating. The character for British hospitality is fittingly maintained by Mr George Stoddard, our Consul, who occupies the palatial residence of a Portuguese noble, and dispenses the duties of his office in a manner that may well reconcile the strictest economist at home to the most inadequate stipend of

and linen, may be procured at a given rate. It is inconceivable what annoyances you are saved by such an arrangement; besides the endless impositions practised upon the ignorance of foreigners by servants and tradesmen, it is no small luxury to be able to pay a given sum down monthly, instead of the interminable daily payments which the ready money system of Madeira requires. Plate, furniture, pianofortes, saddles, guns, and, in fact, any things that are brought out as *luggage*, are allowed to pass through the Custom House free of charge, on the bond of some resident householder being given that the owner of the property will export it in eighteen months. Portuguese servants may be hired for house and kitchen work at the rate of about from four to six dollars per month for the former, and from six to eight dollars for the latter, service. Those who are content with a plain table, average honesty, and moderate attention, have no reason to be dissatisfied. Provisions of all sorts are cheap. English bread, which is sold at $2\frac{1}{2}d$ the pound, is the dearest article of food; the quality of it, however, is excellent. Mutton, which is an indifferent meat, fetches from $3\frac{1}{2}d$ to $4d$ a pound; beef, which is good, from $3\frac{1}{2}d$ to $4d$; and veal, from $4d$ to $5d$. Fowls may be purchased at from $10d$. to $1s.\ 3d$ a couple. The markets are held at daybreak, and all the meat, the best fish, and best fruits are brought at that time. Tea, soap, and tobacco are contraband, but the Custom House is not inexorable. A common English wardrobe, with the addition of a few lighter articles, and a waterproof covering for the mountains, suffice for clothing.—
Harcourt.

£300 a year attached to it; for the obligations are often irksome, if not very onerous; and not a few of them arising out of melancholy occurrences, to whose frequency the tombstones and monuments in the English burial-ground bear such significant testimony. This Anglo *Pere la Chaise* of the Western Atlantic is one of the first objects visited—and, alas! often the last, by the survivors of those whom

> The verdant rising and the flowery hill,
> The vale enamell'd, and the crystal rill,
> The ocean rolling, and the shelly shore,
> Beautiful objects, shall delight no more
> Now the lax'd sinews of the weaken'd eye
> In watery damp and dim suffusion lie

Bidding adieu, however, to these melancholy matters, we again resume our course.

HOTEL, FORMERLY CONVENT, TENERIFFE.

CHAPTER III.

MADEIRA TO CAPE VERDS, WITH A GLANCE AT THE CANARIES.

Oceanic Sailing again.—Halcyon weather, and modern steaming to the *Fortunatæ Insulæ* of the Ancients.—A stave on the saffron-coloured singing birds.—Touching Tenriffe, and Miltonic parallel to the Arch-Enemy.—Approach to Porto Grande, and what we found there, especially its extensive accommodation for steamers.—Deficiency of water the one draw-back.—Something concerning Ethiopic Serenaders under the Line.—Promethean Promontary extraordinary.—A memento of mortality midway in the world.—Portuguese rewards honourably earned by an Englishman.—Utility of Consuls in such places.—First acquaintance with an earthquake.—Verd Grapes soured by a paternal government.—Interchange of news between the Outward and the Homeward bound.—A good propelling turn towards a brother of the screw.

> Or other worlds they seem'd, or Happy Isles,
> Like those Hesperian gardens famed of old,
> Fortunate fields, and groves, and flowery vales,
> Thrice happy isles.—*Paradise Lost, Book iii.*

This track is, generally speaking, about the most pleasant in the Atlantic Ocean; fine sunny weather and fresh north-east trade winds, which blow with tolerable regularity nearly the whole year round, rendering it very easy sailing indeed, and proportionably agreeable to passengers, who may be supposed by this time to have attained their sea-legs. In our case the wind was, unfortunately too light to be of much use, as a vessel going from ten to eleven knots, under steam, must have a very strong breeze to get a-head of such speed and assist the machinery, as well as obtain another knot or two. We pass the Canaries (or Fortunate Isles, as they were called,) to windward, having in view the far-famed Peak of Teneriffe, upheaving high its giant bulk 12,182 feet, and keeping our course direct for St. Vincent. The Canaries are naturally associated with our earliest school-boy notions, as the original home of the charming little universal household songster,[*] to whom they have given their name, but here called thistle-finch, and having for its companions the blackbird, linnet, and others of the same tuneful and now Saxonized family. The real Canary of these islands, however, the *Fringilla Canaria* of Linnæus, and which still abounds here, is not of the saffron or yellow colour it attains in Europe, but is, in its wild state, the

---

[*] Two distinct species of finch (*Carduelis*) appear to have afforded the different varieties of singing bird, familiarly known by this name. The one which is best known in its wild state is the *Carduelis canaria* of Cuvier, and is very abundant in Madeira, where its characters and habits have been observed with much attention by Dr. Heineken. 'It builds,' says this naturalist, 'in thick, bushy, high shrubs and trees, with roots, moss, feathers, hair, &c.; pairs in February, lays from four to six pale blue eggs, and hatches five, and often six times in the season. It is a delightful songster, with, beyond doubt, much of the nightingale's and sky-lark's, but none of the wood-lark's, song.'—'A pure wild song from an island canary, at liberty, in full throat, in a part of the country so distant from the haunts of men that it is quite unsophisticated, is unequalled, in its kind, by any thing I have ever heard in the way of bird-music.' The canary-bird was brought into Europe as early as the 16th century, and is supposed to have spread from the coast of Italy, where a vessel, which was bringing to Leghorn a number of these birds, besides its merchandise, was wrecked. As, however, they were males chiefly which were thus introduced, they were for some time scarce, and it is only of late years that their education and the proper mode of treating them have been known.—*Brande*, 1853.

colour of our common field or grey linnet, the yellow hue being the result of repeated crossings in its artificial state amongst us. The Canaries are amongst several other islands that were known to the ancients, but not discovered by modern Europe until the middle of the fifteenth century, when, after a brave resistance from the natives, the Spaniards conquered and have since retained them.

Though not exactly in the route of the Argentina, nor intended to be touched at by any of the company's vessels, still being comparatively so near the Canaries, and especially of that particular one whereof mention is made by the great English bard, in verse as majestic as the phenomenon he speaks of:

> On the other side, Satan, alarmed,
> Collecting all his might, dilated stood,
> Like Teneriff or Atlas, unremoved
> His stature reach'd the sky, and on his crest
> Sat horror plumed.—Paradise Lost, Book IV

we must present a souvenir of our proximity to so celebrated a vicinage, and we cannot do so in a more graceful or welcome form than the sketch prefixed to this chapter.

The Cape Verds consist of seven principal islands, and were tolerably populous, but of late years have been subjected to a continuous emigration to South America and the West Indies, where, like the hardy mountaineers from Madeira, they are found most useful in tilling the soil, and in other laborious occupations; thus demonstrating the fallacy of the old notion, that laziness is the predominant element in the Spanish and Portuguese idiosyncrasy. What appears to be a present disadvantage, in regard to this human flight from the Verds, may prove beneficial hereafter, when the Ilheos (as they are called) return to their homes, possessed of a little money wherewith to improve their social and moral condition. The islands produce wine, barilla, large quantities of orchilla weed, and cochineal, the cultivation of which is rapidly forming a more and more considerable item of export. Steam navigation will ere long bring them into much closer commercial contact with the world, and enhance the appreciation of their products and natural advantages. The climate is fine, though subject to occasional high temperature and frequent droughts. Despite the name Verds, suggestive of Arcadian animation, nothing can be more desolate than the appearance of the islands, as approached from the sea; bold, high rocks, against which the surge breaks violently, with mountains towering in the clouds, are general characteristics, to which those of the island of St. Vincent offer no exception. On our arrival the weather was thick, with drizzling rain, as we made Porto Grande, and only cleared up in time to enable us to see Bird Island, a most remarkable sugar-loaf rock, standing right in the entrance of the bay, after passing which we reached the anchorage ground in a few minutes. A more convenient little harbour can hardly be imagined, being nearly surrounded with hills (or mountains as they may be called), which protect it from all winds save the westward, where Bird Island stands as a huge beacon, most admirably adapted for a light-house, and on which it is to be hoped one will soon be placed. There is deep water close to the shore on most sides of the bay, that where the town is built being the shallowest; and here some wooden jetties are run out, having very extensive coal and patent fuel *dépôts* close at hand, where these combustibles are put into iron lighters, and sent off to the vessels. So beautifully clear is the water in the bay that you can see the bottom at a depth of from twenty to thirty feet, literally alive with fish of all kinds, but for which the people seem to care very little, either for home consumption or export, though there is no doubt that, in the latter direction, a large business might be done with profitable results.

Porto Grande must become a most important coaling station, situated as it is midway between Europe and South America, and close to the African coast. Several important steam companies have already adopted it, viz., the Royal Mail (Brazil), the General Screw, the Australian, as also the South American, and General Steam Navigation Company, whilst occasional steamers are, likewise, glad to touch at it. At the period of which I am writing, the Great Britain was the last that coaled here, on her way to Australia. In order to meet this increased demand, a proportionate degree of activity and exertion is observable on shore; and a large number of iron lighters, carrying from 15 to 40 tons each, are now in constant requisition, loaded, and ready to be taken alongside the steamers the instant they cast anchor. Unfortunately, there is a very poor supply of water, the want of it having been the occasion of frequent emigration in the history of the islands; but it is understood to be attainable at a slight expense; and a small outlay conjointly made by the steam companies might not only procure a plentiful provision of this all-necessary element, but also other conveniences, essential to the comfort of passengers. There is no doubt that, as the place progresses, supplies of meat, fruit, and vegetables, will be forwarded thither from the neighbouring islands, which are so productive that there is a considerable export of corn; and the cattle are numerous Until lately, fowls were only a penny a piece; and turtles abound. Hitherto there has been no regular marketable demand for such things; but one, and a large one too, is henceforth established, from the causes assigned, and will doubtless be regularly and economically supplied. The labourers here are chiefly free blacks and Kroomen, from the coast of Africa, most of whom speak English, and chatter away at a great rate, as they work in gangs, with a kind of boatswain over them, who uses a whistle to direct their toil—the movements of all the race of Ham to the days of Uncle Tom, being seemingly susceptible of regulation to musical noise of some sort or other; whether the 'concord of sweet sounds,' or what would appear to be such to more refined ears, does not greatly matter.

But for want of vegetation in its neighbourhood, a more picturesque little bay than Porto Grande can hardly be conceived. Towering a short distance above the town, is a kind of table mountain, some 2,500 feet high; and at the opposite side, forming the south-west entrance, is another very lofty one, remarkable as representing the colossal profile of a man lying on his back, *à la* Prometheus. He has his visage towards heaven, wherein there are generally soaring vultures enough to devour him up were he a trifle less tender than volcanic granite. The features are perfect, even to the eyebrows; and a very handsome profile it makes, though it does not appear that any tropical Æschylus has yet converted the material to the humblest legendary, much less epic, purpose. On the shore ground, forming the right side of the bay, looking towards the town, there is a neat little monument, erected to the lamented lady of Colonel Cole, who died here on her way home from India. The spot where she lies is, from its quietude and seclusion, most meet for such a resting-place, there being a small, conical hill behind, with a cottage or two near, and a sprinkling of vegetation on the low ground between, serving to 'keep her memory green' in the mind of many an ocean voyager in his halt at this half-way house between the younger and the elder world.

This little town was thrown back sadly by the epidemic which afflicted it in 1850 and decimated the population. During its continuance Mr. Miller, one of the few English residents, did so much in assisting the inhabitants, as to elicit from the late Queen of Portugal the honour of a knighthood, in one of the first orders in her dominions It requires no small degree of patience and philanthropy to aid the development of a place like this, labouring, as it does, under such great natural difficulties, and where everything has to be brought from a distance, there not being a tree or a blade of grass to be seen—nothing but dry, arid sand, or a burnt-up kind of soil. Undoubtedly, the heat is very great at times; and there are about three months of blowing, rainy weather, which is the only period when vessels might be subjected to inconvenience whilst coaling, as the southerly winds drive up a good deal of sea into the bay. There is an English Consul resident here, Mr. Rendall, who has done much to assist in bringing these islands into notice, and into comparative civilization; and, by so doing, has many times over reimbursed this country in the cost of his stipend of £400 a year, saying nothing of the services he has performed to shipping, in the ordinary discharge of his duties.

Cape Verds are a very numerous family of islands, called after a cape on the African coast (originally named Cabo Verde, or Green Cape, by the Portuguese) to which they lie contiguous, though at a considerable distance from each other in some cases. All are of volcanic formation—one, that of Fogo, or Fuego, once very celebrated as being visible, especially in the night time, at an immense distance at sea. The islands generally do not possess any very attractive points, being unlike Madeira and the Canaries in this respect, as well as in extent of population, that of the latter being four or five times more numerous than the others—say about 200,000 in one, 40,000 in the other case, though some statements make the inhabitants of the Verds considerably more. The islands are occasionally subject to shocks of earthquakes; and there was rather a strong one at Porto Grande the night before we left, supposed on board our vessel to be thunder, from the noise it made, though we were not aware until next day that a shock had been felt on shore. The chief product is salt, a valuable article for vessels trading to South America, though it is here manufactured by the somewhat primitive process of letting the sea-water into the lowlands, where the sun evaporates it. Though Porto Grande, in St. Vincent, is the great place for shipping, and as such almost the only place of interest for passengers in transit, Ribeira Grande, in St. Jago, the principal island, and most southerly of the group, is the chief town, though it is at Porto Playa, (often touched at by ships on the Indian voyage), that the Governor General resides, particularly in the dry season. The island second in importance, in point of size, is St. Nicholas, where are some small manufactories, in the shape of cotton-stuffs, leather, stockings, and other matters. The orchilla weed, however, is the great object of governmental interest, and its monopoly is said to yield some £60,000 per annum; the same wise policy that grasps at that interdicting the manufacture of wine, though grapes grow in profusion, and are of excellent quality for the production of a very acceptable beverage.

Before leaving Porto Grande we had the satisfaction of seeing the General Screw Company's fine vessel, the Lady Jocelyn, arrive on the day she was due from India and the Cape of Good Hope, on her way to Southampton, with mails, and upwards of one hundred passengers. I went on board to give them the latest news from England, which was of course very acceptable, and the columns of the leading journals were eagerly devoured. In exchange I received the 'Cape News,' which did not contain anything very particular, all being quiet there, our old perturbed friend, Sandilli, and his ebonized insurrectionists of the hills having apparently subsided into lilies-of-the-valley of peace and philanthropy. The fine steamers belonging to the General Screw line appeared destined to convey a large portion of passengers between England and India, in preference to the overland route; and, certainly, when one could make the passage in about sixty days, direct, without change of conveyance, and with such splendid accommodation and such conveniences as these vessels afford, it was only natural that they should fill well; and a more comfortable, happy-looking group of passengers I never saw in any vessel.

But, alack for the worthlessness of such moralizings and anticipations as these. This enterprising company have been obliged to abandon their Indian contract, owing to their coaling expenses being out of all proportion to the small sum they received for conveying the mails. The Cape of Good Hope contract, too, will most likely be given up, to the great detriment of that important colony, and at the rate we are progressing, steam communication to Australia does not promise to require the coaling facilities of St. Vincent; still we are of opinion that this island must increase in importance, and that whenever coal freights revert to a moderate scale, steamers will gather there to and from the Southern Ocean.

CHAPTER IV.

CAPE ST. VINCENT TO PERNAMBUCO.—A WORD ON THE CLIMATE OF THE BRAZILS.

Progress from Porto Grande to Pernambuco.—Steam triumphs against adverse wind.—Further Superiority of Screw over Sail.—The Argentina in a South-Wester.—*Apropos* of Malaria, and something sanitary about Brazil.—The yellow fever; whence it comes, and what has become of it?—Quarrels about Quarantine.—Brazil in advance of the old country in these matters.

LEAVING Porto Grande, we shaped our rapid course southwards, to the Brazils, across the wide expanse of ocean lying between the two continents, and in all which prodigious waste of waters there is no port of call nearer than St Helena, latitude, 15 deg 55 min. S., long., 5 44 E, unless we except the turtle-famed Island of Ascension, 800 miles N.E. of the Bonapartean place of exile, which itself is 1,200 miles from the coast of Lower Guinea. The trade winds vary a good deal in their extension towards the line, and in these latitudes commence the difficulties of a sailing ship, which has to deal with calms and variable winds, blowing from all points of the compass, until such time as it catches the southeast trade, and is carried onwards. Our course lay towards Pernambuco, a place I visited for the first time upwards of thirty years back, and where I have often been since, but never in a steamer; and only those who have experienced the difference between the two modes of propulsion, wind alone and steam, can fairly appreciate the value of the latter power. In former years, 40 to 50 days were considered an average passage to Pernambuco, lately reduced to about 30 to 35 by clipper-vessels, whilst a steamer will traverse the distance easily in 20 days, including stoppages to coal, and for any other requisite purpose. The consequence is, that numbers pass to and fro, who would never do so but for the facilities thus afforded, and which afford at the same time a further evidence of the trite truth, already frequently dwelt upon, and which will have to be still more frequently repeated, before we come to a close, that steam navigation becomes the great civilizer of the world, and brings distant nations so much nearer to our own shores.

Our run from St Vincent to Brazil was a very hard one. Losing the trade-wind the day after that on which we left the island, it was replaced by an implacable south-wester, against which our little vessel steamed vigorously, and we could barely carry fore and aft canvas. When, after eight days' tugging we arrived at Pernambuco, there was not an hour's coal left, a consideration which naturally rendered all on board anxious for some short time before. We shaved close past the Island of Fernando de Noronha, showing a conical hill, very like a ship under canvas at a distance. It is a penal settlement of Brazil, and considered very healthy.

Before describing other ports of call on our way to the River Plate, let us just take a glance at the Empire of Brazil, which, from its geographical position, immense fertility and internal resources, is second only in importance to the great Empire of the West—the United States of North America. And, first, in regard to that primal consideration, health, as affected by the climate—a subject on which many years' experience in my own person, and an attentive observation of the health of various classes of Europeans in the tropics enable me to speak with as much weight as should probably attach to the opinion of the majority of non-medical men on a medical topic; and some remarks on that head in the chapter on Pernambuco will probably be found not altogether unworthy of the attention even of the faculty.

Notwithstanding its well-known heat, in common with all other countries within the tropics, and especially a country so large a portion of which is directly beneath the equator, until within the last few years Brazil has been proverbially one of the healthiest climates in the world, and European residents could indulge almost with impunity in the pleasures and luxuries of tropical life. Unfortunately yellow fever has changed all this, and rendered the vital statistics of the harbours and cities of the empire mournful catalogues of suffering and disaster, threatening serious injury to its national prosperity, if the scourge does not soon finally depart from its shores. This, it is devoutly hoped may be the case, and fortunately seems to be so at present, as far as can be augured from the reports now continued for a considerable time. During over thirty years' acquaintance with, and frequent residence in the country, I never experienced or heard of any existing epidemic worthy of the name, or such as could not be readily accounted for, but the aspect of things, at the period of my last arrival, had sadly indeed changed, and the dread pestilence in its ravages seemed to spare neither the hardy European mariner, the native resident, the blacks, nor indeed any class of persons brought within its influence. How or from whence this mysterious visitation had arisen it was impossible to say. Some maintain that it was brought from the coast of Africa, and is a kind of retributive punishment for the iniquitous traffic in human flesh carried on so extensively in the Brazils, until lately, that the government have shown themselves determined to put it down. But those who argue in this fashion forget that the same doctrine would apply in a thousand instances at home and abroad; that the exceptions are unfortunately more numerous than the rule which would be thus set up by human presumption for the admeasurement of the justice of Omniscience; and that it is always imprudent, to say the least of it, to attempt to interpret the causes of such dispensations of Providence by our own notions of human requirement. Others deny the fever to be either epidemic or contagious, affirming that it must be induced by some peculiar atmosphere, generated, no one knows how, on the sea coast; and it certainly is curious enough that vessels have had the sickness on board, whilst coming down the coast, before even touching at a Brazilian port. Whatever be the true cause of this affliction, it ought to teach the Brazilians a lesson not to abuse the bounties of Providence, which they enjoy in almost unexampled profusion, or neglect those means of sanitary protection which are needful even in the healthiest portions of Europe. No doubt much is required to be done in this way, and not in trying to enforce stupid quarantine regulations, which only add to suffering without arresting the arm of the devastator. Indeed, the Brazilian government has shown great good sense in eschewing the absurd formalities in question, therein again exhibiting an immense superiority of intelligence over the mother country; for at Lisbon all the antiquated and superannuated encumbrances and ceremonials are rigorously exacted, though there be not even the shadow of a pretext for enforcing them; for although a ship's bill of health may be perfectly clean, and although the ports she last sailed from may have been long known to be uninfected, still the circumstance of their having been once tainted is sufficient warrant for the Portuguese procrastinators in exacting any amount of detention that may be agreeable to their caprice, whether the vessel be sail or steamer.

THE EMPIRE OF BRAZIL

> "Stern winter smiles on this auspicious clime,
> The fields are florid in eternal prime,
> From the bleak pole no winds inclement blow,
> Mould the round hail, or flake the fleecy snow,
> But from the breezy deep the groves inhale
> The fragrant murmurs of the eastern gale''

CHAPTER V.

EMPIRE OF BRAZIL.

Rather prefatory and not very particular, though somewhat personal — Books on Brazil should be in *Medium Viam* for the present route, avoiding the Scylla of extreme succinctness and the Charybdis of needless diffuseness —Object of the Author to attain the golden medium —With what success, gentle reader, say ?—Discovery of the country by the Portuguese Their subsequent disputes with, and final expulsion of the Dutch —Extent and Population; variety of soil and produce —Difficulty of communication between the provinces and the capital, in consequence of extreme distance and imperfect means of travelling —Extraordinary instance of the roundabout nature of news circulating in Brazil some time ago —Steam corrective of such sluggishness —A glance at the Brazilian littoral, beginning with the Amazon, and ending with Rio Grande do Sul —Para and its productions —Rio Negro, and its recent political elevation —Maranham and its Mercantile importance —Land's steam leveller, on the singular stream of the Itapecuru —Justice for England by Maranham Magistrates —Piauhy and its products, also Ceara, Rio Grande do Norte, and Paraiba —Pernambuco revisited by the writer, and welcomed with a rhythmetical sentimental something concerning 'Long, long, ago!'

LET not the reader suppose, from the heading of this chapter, 'Empire of Brazil,' that he is going to encounter either a dilution or a condensation of Southey, Kidder, Weech, Mawe, Prince Adalbert, St. Hilaire, and others, who have written at great length and in many languages, on so fertile and so expansive a theme. The object of the author in this portion of the volume is merely, by presenting at a glance the position and condition of Brazil generally, to enable those who accompany him in these pages the more readily to recognize the points he is about to put hereafter as the result of his own experience, more especially with reference to the machinery of commercial matters in Brazil. It is often the fault of men very full of a particular subject themselves to take for granted that the public either know a very great deal, or wish to know everything about it. Brazil has suffered much from both these causes in European, and especially in English estimation. Those familiar with and competent to write about it, have either presumed that the public were nearly as wise as themselves, and have passed over matters of great interest. believing them to be stale and exhausted, and dwelling upon the trivialities of personal travel by way of varying a beaten track :—or, on the other hand, the exhaustive process has been applied, and historic and topographic disquisition have been employed with a minuteness that would be only tolerated in English county gazetteers or family chronicles. The consequence is that all but the student or the virtuoso in such matters have been repelled from their perusal. When the idea of writing this book occurred to the author—an idea suggested by frequent inquiries for works that should, in a brief compass, give a tolerable notion of things to be met with and that ought to be known in a route of yearly increasing importance between two quarters of the globe—it was suggested that he should steer between the two extremes just indicated. He has endeavoured to do so; and without further circumlocution, he places before the reader the means of deciding with what success.

Brazil,* as already noticed, was discovered by Cabral on his way to India in 1500 (although it has been asserted that the coast was visited by Martin Belem in 1484) who at first supposed it to be a

* Brazil, as before stated, was originally so named from its valuable dye-wood, called Braziletto or 'Cisalpina Braziletto,' or Pernambuco, Wood of Saint Martha, or Sapan, according to the place which produces it, and by Linnæus, Cæsalpinia custa, which was for many years the richest dye in Europe, and from which the famous Turkey red colours were produced, rivalling the ancient Tyrian purple, and, like it, passing into oblivion, after vast popularity, for other drugs having been substituted, Brazil wood became comparatively little used. It was a close monopoly of the government, who derived a large revenue from its sale, from £100 a ton upwards being the current price in London, and only 8 years ago 4,500 tons were imported into Great Britain. Brazil timber also possesses qualities not generally known, one of which is mentioned by Sir W. G. Ouseley, and accounts for the infrequency of conflagrations in some of the cities of South America, as compared with what happens in the northern portion of the continent, where fire brigades are among the most prominent institutions of the country, and yet do not by any means prevent the mischief they are meant to guard against. He says :—'A proof of the incombustible nature of Brazil wood was afforded at this house (the Mangueiras) previous to my arrival at Rio de Janeiro, when it was occupied by Baron Palencia, at that time Russian Minister to the Imperial Court. One night an attempt was made to set fire to the outside door-like shutters of one of the windows, with a view, doubtless, to getting into and robbing the apartments. In the morning was discovered a heap of still smoking, combustible materials, partially consumed, applied to the outside of the shutter, the planks of which were little injured, although their surface was charred, as the fire had been in actual contact with the wood probably for some hours.' Brazil wood (the dye now so called) is very small sized—sticks, comparatively speaking,—and is not used at all for building purposes, being much too valuable. The ordinary timber of the country is of quite another description.

large island on the coast of Africa.* The reports as to her mineral wealth not being at that time encouraging, little progress was made in colonizing Brazil until 1542, when the Portuguese rulers sent out Thomas de Souza as first governor, who built San Salvador, (or Bahia, as it is now called, capital of the province of the same name,) and materially aided the mission of the Jesuits in civilizing the Indian population. This Portuguese possession was afterwards disputed both by the Spaniards and the Dutch, and the latter succeeded in appropriating several of the northern provinces, viz..—Ceara, Seregipe, Pernambuco, and Bahia, which they held for a considerable time during the 17th century, and did much towards the permanent prosperity of the country, by building forts, enlarging towns, and carrying out a number of useful public works, which remain as monuments of their laboriousness and perseverance to this day, especially in the capitals of the two last-named provinces. Much gallantry and patriotism were shown by the native Brazilian and Portuguese residents in their conflict with the Hollanders, ending in the final expulsion of the latter from the entire coast, although this event may be considered a misfortune to the country itself, in losing so industrious and painstaking a race.

The Brazilian empire extends from about 4 degrees north, to 33 degrees south, latitude; its extreme length is from 2,500 to 2,600 miles, and breadth above 2,000 at the widest part, it contains some 2,500,000 square miles of territory, comprising every variety of soil and culture, and is possessed of considerable variety of climate. Its population has been variously estimated at from six

* Of the simultaneousness of these discoveries, Humboldt says:—'The course of great events, like the results of natural phenomena, is ruled by eternal laws, with few of which we have any perfect knowledge. The fleet which Emanuel, King of Portugal, sent to India, under the command of Pedro Alvarez Cabral, on the course discovered by Gama, was unexpectedly driven on the coast of Brazil on the 22nd April, 1500. From the zeal which the Portuguese had manifested since the expedition of Diaz in 1487, to circumnavigate the Cape of Good Hope, a recurrence of fortuitous circumstances, similar to those exercised by oceanic currents on Cabral's ships, could hardly fail to manifest itself. The African discoveries would thus probably have brought about that of America south of the Equator; and thus Robertson was justified in saying that it was decreed in the destinies of mankind that the new continents should be made known to European navigators before the close of the fifteenth century.'

to seven millions; but no data exist from which one can form more than an approximate calculation. Out of this number, one half may be set down as slaves, and the other half mixed races, from the native-born Portuguese downwards to the pure Indian. One of the great draw-backs hitherto experienced in administering the government of the Brazils has been the distance of the towns and provinces from the metropolis, Rio Janeiro, and this has more especially applied to the northern provinces, from Para to Pernambuco, where, owing to the almost constant prevalence of a northerly current, sailing-vessels took a very long time in getting down the coast; so that, in the absence of communication by land, the intelligence of disturbances or temporary rebellion only reached the seat of government a considerable period after the first outbreak. An extraordinary and almost incredible instance of this occurred on the occasion of the formidable revolt of the province of Para, the first news of which was received at Rio Janeiro by way of England, sixty days after a British sailing ship had left Para, and another recrossed the Atlantic, and anchored in the port of the Brazilian capital, no ship, within all that period, having been able to make way from Para to Rio against the monsoon and current and wind that prevails for a great part of the year, blowing from the antarctic circle towards the equator. Perhaps the astonishment created by this state of things will, however, be triflingly mitigated if the reader will bear in mind that Brazil is as large as nearly a dozen Great Britains; and will also recollect what vagueness, incertitude, and delay characterise the receipt of intelligence in London from Constantinople and St Petersburgh, notwithstanding special steamers, express trains, electric telegraphs, government couriers, and time-and-space-annihilating editors of innumerable newspapers, at both ends and all along the whole line of operations. Steam navigation has however in a great measure remedied this evil, as it has done so many others; and news is now regularly transmitted between Rio Janeiro and Para by a steam company, liberally subsidized by the government, the former being bound to dispatch a vessel once a fortnight, calling at all the ports In the absence of internal roads or communications along the coast, steam must very properly be regarded as the main-stay of the executive, at the same time that it offers the needful facility for provincial deputies attending the sittings of the Rio chambers. Steam, valuable everywhere, is invaluable here, and may, indeed, be looked upon as the great civilizer and regenerator of a country like Brazil, with a sea-coast extending nearly 4,000 miles from north to south; while other tributary lines of steamers are being established in the innumerable bays and rivers. The northernmost point is the mighty Amazon, which is being explored and opened to general traffic by another steam company, established at Rio Janeiro, and likewise aided with an ample subsidy from the government; though from the terms in which certain North American and other writers, to some of whom we shall have to allude hereafter, speak of the Brazilian authorities, it might be inferred that not a particle of enterprise of this kind is tolerated, much less encouraged. Considering that it is only 20 years since the first funnel darkened the Brazilian waters, this wonder-working agent of steam may fairly be said to be only in its infancy, and its progeny will no doubt ere long be greatly multiplied on the coast and up the vast fluvial arteries of the empire. A brief glance along the littoral boundaries of this almost boundless dominion will soon shew the transcendent importance of steam to such a region. The northernmost province of the Brazils is

Para, with a capital of the same name, otherwise called Belem, situated on the north-eastern bank of the Amazon, 80 miles from its entrance. From the cause already assigned (distance from the seat of government) the progress of this important province, containing upwards of a million square miles, much of which is yet unknown, has been greatly retarded by civil wars and an unruly population. Its chief productions are corn, caoutchouc (or gum elastic), ipecacuanha, nuts, &c.; but there is no doubt that the navigation of the Amazon will lead to great additional sources of export, and soon render this province one of the most flourishing in the empire, as its immense fertility, miscellaneous produce, and the incalculable advantages of having the greatest river in the world traversing its entire length, so well entitle it to be. The population, of whom some ten thousand are probably Indians, amounts to about 350,000. Of their condition, and that of the province and its capital, we shall speak in detail under the head of the Amazon; as also of

Rio Negro, an internal province situated on the Amazon, and communicating with the seaport of Para. It has only lately been raised to the dignity of a province.

Maranhao, or *Maranham,* or *San Luiz,* follows on the line of sea-coast, with a large, well-built capital, similarly named, but is not very densely populated, containing probably not more than a quarter of a million inhabitants to an area of nearly 70,000 square miles, the soil being well watered and fertile, and, like nearly the whole of the Brazilian empire, producing wood of the finest kind for almost every purpose. It has always been looked upon as a steady-going place, although its progress has not kept pace with other more favoured provinces to the southward. Its chief production is cotton, of which the export is considerable, averaging about 30,000 bags per annum, and rice and sarsaparilla also form considerable items. The town is situated on an island, some 30 miles from the coast, with rather a dangerous navigation to it. though of easy access for small vessels, a couple of forts defending the entrance. It is said to contain a population of 30,000, which is probably an exaggeration. Its buildings, however, are on a scale not unworthy of such numbers, and consist of a theatre, hospital, several convents, and schools of a very superior order. About 200 miles up the River Itapicuru is the important town of Caxias, formerly Aldeas Altas, and which, though suffering itself considerably in the civil wars of 1838-40, has nearly double the population of Maranham. Its connection with the latter has been greatly accelerated by means of a small steamer running between the two places, and called the Caxiense, built by the constructor of the Argentina, Mr. John Laird, of Birkenhead, under peculiar reservation as to her draught of water; which was not to be more than three feet, and even this appears too much for the shallow places in the river during the dry season, though she seems to have been eminently successful in other respects, and of great utility, not only in going up and down the river with freight and passengers, but also in towing vessels and small craft. The scenery on the Itapicuru is described as most romantic, the banks being high, and lined with towering trees, in many places almost meeting across. The navigation however is very uncertain and irregular, as will have been inferred from what we have said of the necessity of exceedingly shallow-bottomed steamers, in the dry season, when there is not more than from two to three feet of water in some places, whilst in the rainy season it will rise to 20 or 30 feet, inundating, or rather irrigating, the country round to some extent, and rendering it, like the Delta of the Nile, and for the same reason, uncommonly fertile, so much so, indeed, as to leave little scope for industry; for, by merely striking a few plants in the mud, two or three crops a-year can be obtained, more than sufficient for the wants of the inhabitants. On the banks of the river are many large fazendas, or estates, where cotton only was formerly grown, but they are now trying sugar likewise, and with encouraging assurance of remunerative results.

Ascending the river, the first important place arrived at is the Villa de Rosario, situated in a fertile district, and where many influential planters reside. Next in rotation are Paioul and St. Nicholas; afterwards, there comes Itapicaru-Merim, where vessels, drawing 4 feet of water can go in the driest season; but beyond the latter-named place, not more than two feet and a half. Nearly all the produce shipped at Maranham comes down this river in canoes, of about 40 tons register, carrying 300 bags of cotton; and in the dry season this voyage will take three months to perform what the steamer does now in less than four days! In the rainy season these river craft will come down much more quickly; but the average time then occupied in going up is still greater, owing to the strength of the freshes in the river, the vessel having to be hauled up by bodily force, ropes being taken from tree to tree, and requiring a crew for the purpose. This slight sketch of the difficulties attending the navigation of one of the internal rivers of the Brazils by native craft, will show what may be effected by steam, even under the most unfavourable circumstances of a very shallow stream; and what may we not expect from such a communication being established along the mighty Amazon?

Maranham was a short time back the scene of a most brutal murder of an English resident; and, to the credit of the local government, four of the miscreants concerned in it were hanged, the force of which observation will be understood by those who know the difficulty of administering justice in a country like Brazil, where, owing to the vast distance of one town from another, and the consequent difficulty of sustaining the vigilance of pursuit, and the facilities for baffling it, crimes of this nature may be expected to go long unpunished, if the perpetrators be not caught almost red-handed in the very deed of blood. The acting President of Maranham is represented as most energetic and efficient, having done much to improve the town and maintain civil order in his district. His official residence is a very fine one, and should have been mentioned among the imposing structures of the town, or rather city, for such Maranham is, at least in the English sense of the term, being the residence of a bishop, and containing an episcopal palace of considerable dimensions, and of striking architectural appearance. The place, and some of its people, still retain slight traces of its French origin, having been founded by that nation, as late as the end of the 17th century; and, it is said, that that language is better spoken in Maranham than in any other part of Brazil, the capital itself not excepted.

Piauhy.—Beyond Maranham lies the little province of this name, which has no port or outlet; but in the district of Parahyba, 100 miles to the eastward of Maranham, are extensive plains, extending over 6,000 square miles, watered by numerous rivers and covered with cattle, which can be bought exceedingly cheap. Much carne seca (dried beef) is cured here and sent to

Maranham, as well as cattle, in beautiful condition. It is easy to imagine what an important element of supply this will be to other parts of the empire not so well provided, so soon as better means of transit exist. Unlike most other portions of Brazil, Piauhy is deficient in wood; but, in addition to its fine pastures, it produces in great abundance maize, millet, sugar, rice, cotton, jalap, ipecacuanha, and some silver, iron, and lead, but none of these yield anything like what may be expected when there is a population something better proportioned to the area we have named, for at present the inhabitants do not exceed 70,000. Its capital, Oeyras, has but about 3,000 inhabitants, but contains some remarkable ecclesiastical evidences of the former presence of the Jesuits.

Ceara is a very sandy district, but with a good back country where many cattle are bred, but which suffers much from occasional drought. Ceara exports a fair quantity of hides, some cotton, and fustic. The town of Aracati is situated on a picturesque river, but with a very bad bar entrance, on which several vessels have been lost; they, therefore, now generally load outside, some miles higher up the coast, where an indent admits of shelter, and to which the cotton is taken in jangadas (native craft.) Though the heat in this province is excessive in summer, the climate is nevertheless healthy. Its population is somewhat about 200,000; and gold, as well as copper, iron, and salt, is among its yet very imperfectly ascertained mineral resources. The town of Ceara is quite on the coast, and has no harbour, or protection, beyond a reef of rocks that forms a kind of breakwater, within which vessels can ride at anchor. It is a curious thing that the reef, of which this constitutes a part, extends along nearly the whole coast of Brazil, from Cape St. Roque to the Abrolhos, near Rio Janeiro, and is of the same hard coral nature. In many places an entrance through, or a break in the reef, enables vessels to get to small ports inside, and jangadas can sail along the coast, within these reefs for hundreds of miles, entirely protected from the sea, which rolls in and breaks upon them with a deafening noise.

Rio Grande do Norte, a name derived from the river which, after an east course, enters the Atlantic at Natal, its capital, possesses a good harbour, but has little direct trade, procuring its supplies chiefly from Pernambuco. Compared with any of the provinces already spoken of, it is well peopled, there being about 140,000 inhabitants to 32,000 square miles. A few cargoes of Brazil wood were formerly shipped here, being the best quality produced in the whole empire, and prized accordingly, till it fell into disrepute from the causes we have already specified, in speaking of that once-prized ingredient in the art of dyeing. Like Piauhy, Rio Grande do Norte is favourable to cattle-rearing, but exports of that kind, in the shape of hides, tallow, or jerked beef are scanty, because of the paucity of means of transport.

Paraiba is a very fertile province, bordering on that of Pernambuco, and vastly better peopled than the one last described, as it has a population of 70,000 to an area of 9,000 square miles, and cattle of European breeds are raised in considerable numbers with great facility. There is a fine river, some 20 miles in length, leading up to the town, of the same name as the province, where vessels can load alongside the trapixes. The bar entrance is rather intricate, but there is very good anchorage just inside. Paraiba exports largely of cotton, and also of sugar and hides. The upper city is extensive, with large, well-built houses; while the lower, or commercial part of the town, is also extremely good, possessing a splendid Government warehouse, and the whole indicating quondam prosperity, as well as affording additional proof of the industry and perseverance of the Dutch, who formerly held this province in conjunction with Pernambuco. The treasury, in particular, is considered a very fine building; its educational establishments are also excellent; and in the neighbourhood of the town are some of the best-managed coffee plantations probably in the empire.

Pernambuco.—We now approach the most flourishing and remarkable province in the Brazils, upon which the writer hopes he may be pardoned if he descant at some length, as a place inti-

Lightning Source UK Ltd.
Milton Keynes UK
UKHW011153240521
384279UK00007B/1630